HOUSE —OF— DAVID

A BIBLE STUDY

AN INTERACTIVE JOURNEY
TOWARD GOD'S OWN HEART

GREG LAURIE

WITH KAYLEY RIVERA THOMPSON

150 YEARS STRONG

DAVID C COOK

HOUSE OF DAVID (A BIBLE STUDY)
Published by David C Cook
4050 Lee Vance Drive
Colorado Springs, CO 80918 U.S.A.

Integrity Music Limited, a Division of David C Cook
Brighton, East Sussex BN1 2RE, England

DAVID C COOK®, the graphic circle C logo and related marks are registered trademarks of David C Cook.

The website addresses recommended throughout this book are offered as a resource
to you. These websites are not intended in any way to be or imply an endorsement
on the part of David C Cook, nor do we vouch for their content.

All Scripture quotations are taken from the Holy Bible, New Living Translation,
copyright © 1996, 2015 by Tyndale House Foundation. Used by permission of
Tyndale House Publishers, Carol Stream, Illinois 60188. All rights reserved.
The author has added italics to Scripture quotations for emphasis.

ISBN 978-0-8307-8961-0
eISBN 978-0-8307-8962-7

The Team: Michael Covington, Jeff Gerke, Stephanie Bennett, Judy Gillispie,
Karissa Silvers, Jason Jones, James Hershberger, Susan Murdock
Cover Design: Brian Mellema
Cover photography © 2025 Amazon Content Services LLC

Printed in the United States of America
First Edition 2025

1 2 3 4 5 6 7 8 9 10

020725

CONTENTS

INTRODUCTION

Welcome to *House of David: A Bible Study*. Come on in. Kick off your shoes, and hang up your coat. Take a seat on the couch, and pull out your Bible. Together, we're going to learn about a man who made both massive mistakes and excellent choices that changed the course of history for God's people. Don't get too comfy, though, because as we examine the structure of David's life, you're going to find yourself on the edge of your seat, blown away by how God used an ordinary shepherd boy to do extraordinary things.

Here are the main questions we're aiming to answer in this Bible study: Who is David? How does the way he built his life on God help us better understand how to construct our own legacy?

Who is this Bible study for? All of us.

Where are we going? We'll journey from David's calling through his kingship. Encountering David as a young boy who believed in a big God will inspire us to be zealous, and as we reflect on his legacy, we'll dwell on what it means to be wise. In between, we'll discuss David's rough rise to fame, his sins and struggles, and God's redemptive power in his life. Our ultimate goal is to develop a love for the God of David and His Word that transforms our lives, a love that we will pass down to generations to come.

We'll soon discover that, like David, we build the house we live in. We can lay a great foundation by placing our faith in God, making wise choices, loving our family and friends, asking for and offering forgiveness, and seeking hope. We set biblically based fundamentals as our pillars, and we nail our blessings to the walls. While our life-house can seem solid, storms hit and shake the timbers. Sins chip away at the paint. Hardships and hurts cause us to want to lock the front door, turn the light off, and hide.

By visiting the house of David, we can examine how he built his life on God. If we pay close attention, we will walk away with a blueprint for how, through every high and low, to remain, rebuild, and revive our own God-given callings.

In exploring the life of our main character, we'll use filmmaking terms from the set of the Prime Video series *House of David* to guide us through our Bible study. Within these pages you'll find the following recurring elements.

Close-Up

A close-up is when the camera zooms in on a specific character. These sections will challenge you to take a close look at your life through personal application questions and practices. The God who was with David is the same God who is with us, which means He has lessons for us to learn from David's life story. Take the time to dig deep, open your heart, and ask God to speak directly to you. Respond however you see fit—write a response, doodle in the margins, and get creative.

Foreshadowing

From cover to cover, the Bible tells the story of God's redemptive plan to save His people. While we read about David, it's vital we see that his legacy was ultimately pointing to the great King who would come to save us all. In these sections, you will notice how God used the life of David to foretell Jesus' coming and calling. As you read the referenced Scriptures, note parallels between the Old and New Testaments. Stand in awe of the way God has been threading His plan to care for us and bring us in as sons and daughters throughout the tapestry of history.

Director's Cut

In this version of a film or show, the director shares their original intent. It's typically released apart from the version released in theaters. In our study, we'll use these sections to offer additional information or situational context that can help you better understand David's story and my thoughts as the author.

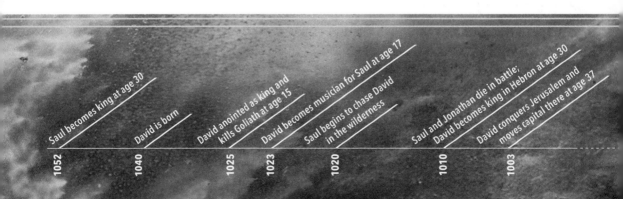

Saul becomes king at age 30

David is born

David anointed as king and kills Goliath at age 15

David becomes musician for Saul at age 17

Saul begins to chase David in the wilderness

Saul and Jonathan die in battle; David becomes king in Hebron at age 30

David conquers Jerusalem and moves capital there at age 37

1052   1040   1025   1023   1020   1010   1003

Breaking the Fourth Wall

This is a term for when an actor looks right at the camera and acknowledges the audience. This breaks the invisible barrier between the medium and the spectator. In our case, we're going to sit down with David at key points in lessons and hear his insights. Look at his questions, and answer them as extensively as you can. The more you share and learn, the more God can use this study to open your eyes and expand your heart.

Character Introductions

When someone new steps onstage in David's story, we will take a moment to get to know a few of their key character traits and discover their role in David's life. As you meet them, think about what it would have been like to greet them in person. Use your imagination to allow these characters to come to life.

Props

In a movie, props are items used in a scene, like a telephone, cane, or book. In this study, *props* refers to graphical elements such as maps, objects, or photos that illustrate something from David's life.

David's Diary

David was a poet and musician. He walked out his faith practices and wrote more than seventy of the psalms in the Bible. In effect, they were David's diary. In our "David's Diary" sections, we will take one of David's psalms that is relevant to our lesson and break it down using the practices of slowly reading, reflecting, absorbing, and praying. Simply follow the instructions provided. This is a starting point for you to have your own conversation with God; borrow the words I have suggested, or create your own. Use David's Diary to allow the new knowledge and insights you've gained to sink into your heart, and apply them to your relationship with God.

Personal Psalm Writing

Using David's writings as a template, you'll wrap up each lesson by creating your own personal psalm. These will serve as your way to summarize everything you've learned in each lesson, record what God is doing in your life now, and create an expectation for the upcoming lesson.

Solomon is born when David is 41

David dies at age 70; Solomon becomes king at age 29

Solomon begins building the temple

Temple completed

Solomon dies

999

970

967

960

931

Scripture

The Bible verses in this study are taken from the New Living Translation (NLT) of the Bible. It is one of the most popular modern Bible translations in the world and uses everyday English, making it easy for all of us to understand. Please feel free to look up any of these verses on your own in your favorite Bible translation.

With the *House of David* series, devotional book, and (now) Bible study, I pray the legacy of David will come alive for you. May you use all these tools to place yourself right into David's shoes and ask, "What would I have done in that situation? How is God using this ancient story to speak to me in the present?" Utilize every paragraph and page of this Bible study to write, reflect, and talk to God so that you, too, can start crafting a legacy that transforms your family and community with the love of Jesus.

The door to David's house is wide open. Are you ready? Let's walk in.

A MAN AFTER GOD'S OWN HEART

Lion of the Tribe of Judah, your heart seeks after
God, and therefore He has sought after you.

SAMUEL, SEASON 1, EPISODE 3, HOUSE OF DAVID

The LORD has sought out a man after his
own heart. The LORD has already appointed
him to be the leader of his people.

1 SAMUEL 13:14

WHO WAS DAVID?

Years ago, when my son Christopher was little, he had a plastic tugboat toy that he played with in the swimming pool. He enjoyed the challenge of trying to submerge his unsinkable boat. He would take it to the bottom of the pool and hold it down, only to discover that no matter how many times he tried, it always bobbed right back up to the surface.

After a number of years, when he was past the point of being entertained by floating toys, I said to him, "Christopher, would you like to get fireworks and blow up the tugboat now?" He was a boy, so of course his answer was "Yes!"

Executing our well-thought-out plan for an explosion, I cut a little hole in the top and dropped a cherry bomb—a spherical firework that looks like a cherry with a long fuse for the stem—into the hull of the ship. (If cherry bombs are illegal where you live, please don't tell anyone we did this.) Then we put the little tugboat in the middle of the pool. We were both filled with childlike excitement as I lit the firework and dropped the boat into the pool.

We watched wide-eyed for what would happen next. Would it skyrocket to outer space? Would the boat be blown to bits? To our surprise, the plastic was so thick that the "explosion" could barely be heard. The toy didn't get blown to smithereens, but Christopher did finally succeed in making that thing sink. While we had set out to discover how to blow a toy to pieces, the lesson we actually learned was that the best way to make something sink is to poke a hole in it.

That can happen with our spiritual ship as well.

It's often gradual, not overnight, that we find ourselves heading toward rock bottom. We may not even notice it's happening. We intended to have a life of fireworks, shining with God-given goals and dreams. We don't notice when a little compromise here, a lowering of the guard there, and an allowance for sin somewhere else begin to effectively poke holes in our souls. Before we know it, we are taking on water.

As we look at the life of David, we'll examine our own lives as well. Write down any specific ways you have been "taking on water" in the following areas:

AREAS	TAKING ON WATER
Relational	
Mental	
Spiritual	
Physical	
Emotional	
Other	

This brings us to our main character.

David was a man who was always either sailing or sinking. He was having a mountaintop moment or crying out to God from the valley. He conquered Goliath in his most well-known victory and caved in to temptation when he saw Bathsheba in his greatest defeat. He rose from living in complete obscurity to having hit songs written about him. Despite his extreme ups and downs, the thing that stands out most about David is that he was a true believer. Whenever he turned away from the Lord, he didn't stay there. Anytime he sank his spiritual ship, he looked to God to bring him back up to the surface.

DAVID
shepherd boy
brave & skilled fighter
second king of Israel
musician & poet

David was a rough outcast and warrior who became the king of Israel. Simultaneously, he was a shepherd boy, musician, and poet. In fact, they still sing about David in Israel today in a little folk song that goes, "David, David, melech Yisrael," meaning, "David, David (is) king of Israel."[1]

While we will explore much about this multifaceted man in the pages to come, the main things you need to know are (1) David was the greatest king that Israel ever had and (2) he is a member of the messianic family tree, the fourteen-times great-grandfather of Jesus Christ Himself. This connection is mentioned in the Gospels.

As you write down the text of the verses in the following chart, also note David's connection to Jesus.

REFERENCE	VERSE	DAVID'S CONNECTION TO JESUS
Matthew 1:1		
Matthew 9:27		
Luke 1:32		

David is one of the main characters of the whole Bible. Not only is he related to Christ, but the New Testament also references him fifty-nine times, and sixty-six chapters of the Old Testament were written by or dedicated to him.[2] This grand list makes David seem like an incredible man and leader, a spotless paragon of virtue and holiness. Tragically, just like us, he was far from it. David was also an adulterer, a murderer, and a liar.

As we examine his story, we will see that the real testimony of his life is not that he was naturally great but that God called an ordinary man and gave him a second chance. What made David's legacy so remarkable wasn't that he was a macho dude collecting trophies for all the victories he won (though he did win many) but that he was tender toward God. David is the only man described in the Bible as "a man after [God's] own heart" (1 Sam. 13:14).

So, how did this all happen? How did an unfavored shepherd boy in a field become a mighty king? Let's find out.

THE KING AFTER THE PEOPLE'S HEART

In film, an establishing shot is typically the opening visual in a movie or TV show that helps the viewer understand the setting. It is often a wide shot that reveals the landscape, the weather, or time of day, plus which characters are present. This shot sets the mood and tone for the following scene. This section is an establishing shot of the life of David, where we'll gather all the knowledge we need to understand what led up to David's anointing as king.

First, it's vital that we know that while David was the best king Israel ever had, he was not the first. During the three-century span between the end of Israel's conquest of the Holy Land and 1 Samuel 10, judges and prophets guided the people. At the moment in Israel's history when our Bible study

BREAKING THE FOURTH WALL

Brother or sister, I am so glad you've made it here to me, David, and this Bible study. Before we dive into my life, let's take a moment to dream and believe in God for big things. As you'll soon find out, I was always a bit of a dreamer, and I discovered that God can really do anything. He's not intimidated by your hopes *or* your fears. So lay it all out there as you answer the following questions:

What are you hoping to get out of this Bible study?

What is something you've already learned about me that you didn't know before?

As "a man after God's own heart," I know this phrase carries a lot of weight. Does the notion of becoming a man or a woman after God's heart excite you? Does it feel impossible? Seem aspirational? Frustrate you? A little of all the above?

picks up, God's people were being led by the aging prophet Samuel. The people decided they had a better idea than God's plan: they asked God to give them a king just like every other nation had. So He essentially said, "All right. If that's really what you want, I'll give you a king."

Let's zoom out to see the context of the story David stepped into by reading the following verses. As you study, record as many details as you can about how Israel came to desire a king.

1 Samuel 10:17–27

SAMUEL
Israel's last judge
prominent prophet
great man of faith

Into our story enters Saul, the first king of Israel. On paper, this new king looked pretty good. Saul was handsome. He appeared to be humble. He was tall and imposing. He stood out from other men. He even started out quite well as king. But it was only a matter of time before it became clear how thin-skinned, paranoid, jealous, and self-destructive he could be. (Maybe he was showing his true colors when he hid behind the suitcases! See 1 Samuel 10:21–22.) The people had rejected God as king, so He gave them a king after their own heart, not a king after His.

Things started to take a turn for the worst when Saul directly disobeyed God's orders before a battle between the Israelites (God's people) and their enemy, the Philistines. Samuel had given Saul clear directions: "Then go down to Gilgal ahead of me. I will join you there to sacrifice burnt offerings and peace offerings. You must wait for seven days until I arrive and give you further instructions" (1 Sam. 10:8).

SAUL
first king of Israel
great military leader
rebelled against God

A whole week went by, and Samuel appeared to be a no-show. Saul and his army got sick of waiting, so the king took matters into his own hands.

Read 1 Samuel 13:7–14, and fill in the blanks:

Some of them crossed the _____ and escaped into the land of Gad and Gilead.

Meanwhile, Saul stayed at Gilgal, and his men were _____ _____. Saul waited there seven days for Samuel, as Samuel had instructed him earlier, but Samuel still didn't come. Saul realized that his troops were rapidly slipping away. So he demanded, "Bring me the burnt offering and the peace offerings!" And Saul sacrificed the burnt offering himself.

Just as Saul was finishing with the burnt offering, Samuel arrived. Saul went out to meet and welcome him, but Samuel said, "_____ _____?"

Saul replied, "I saw my men scattering from me, and you didn't arrive when you said you would, and the Philistines are at Micmash ready for battle. So I said, 'The Philistines are ready to march against us at Gilgal, and I haven't even asked for the LORD's help!' So I felt compelled to offer the burnt offering myself before you came."

"How _____!" Samuel exclaimed. "You have not kept _____ the LORD your God gave you. Had you kept it, the LORD would have established your kingdom over Israel forever. But now your kingdom must end, for the LORD has sought out _____ _____. The LORD has already appointed him to be the leader of his people, because you have not kept the LORD's command."

Saul proved himself unworthy, so God sought out a man after His own heart. Where have we heard that before? Ah, yes. David. Into the picture steps a shepherd boy about to be called out of the field and onto the throne.

CLOSE-UP

Oh, Saul. While it's easy to blame him, we can have compassion too.

Do you find yourself sympathizing with "the king after the people's heart"? Do you ever find yourself, like Saul, struggling to wait on God? Why do you think waiting is so hard?

Saul discovered there were big consequences for taking action in his own timing rather than God's. Have you ever experienced the consequences of choosing your way over God's? What happened?

Describe a time when the waiting was worth it.

Write down some of the things you are waiting for. Underneath your list, write "THE WAIT IS WORTH IT" in capital letters.

THE KING AFTER GOD'S HEART

I love the expression "a man after my own heart." We use it a lot. If I see some guy chowing down on a big burger, I'll say, "Now that's a man after my own heart." What does that mean? It means that guy reminds me of myself a little bit, right? He loves what I love.

So the Lord said, "I love David. He reminds Me of My own nature and character. He desires what I desire." What a compliment! The Lord saw the potential in David, so He chose him as the next king of Israel. He commanded Samuel to go to a little town called Bethlehem to anoint the next king. In complete obedience, Samuel set out with only the clue that the future ruler would be one of the sons of Jesse. It's in the middle of this quest for a new king that David enters the story.

Open your Bible to 1 Samuel 16:1–3, and answer the following questions:

What did the Lord say to Samuel?

Where was God sending him?

What were Samuel's instructions?

Who was Samuel told to anoint?

Here's what's so interesting: Though Samuel was in the exact place God directed him to go, he still didn't have any clue who the next king would be. *God leads us one step at a time.*

As I look back on my own life, I wish I could tell you that everything happened just as I planned. But it almost never does, does it? God just gives us His Word to

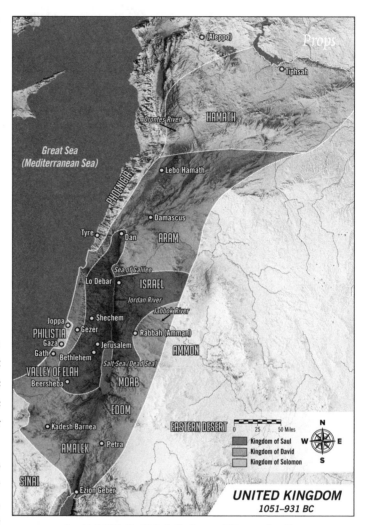

Copyright © 2025 by David C Cook. All rights reserved. Map image adapted from Getty Images, copyright © 2021 Frank Ramspott/iStock /Getty Images Plus.

DIRECTOR'S CUT: WHAT WE CAN LEARN FROM SAMUEL

Samuel teaches us that when we don't know what direction God is calling us to go in, we should simply obey whatever God has already told us to do: Read the Bible every day. Have a prayer life. Call out to and

listen to the Lord. When we do what we already know God wants us to do, the Lord will, in His timing, show us what to do next.

If you feel like you're stuck or haven't heard from God about where to go, here are three directions you can always move:

Back Up—You can always go back to a place God has called you into previously. Maybe this means returning to the church you grew up in to seek community, going through this Bible study (or another) with old friends and restarting a group, or serving in a role or place you know God has asked you to before. Sometimes

follow, and it's up to us to be obedient one step at a time. *God's way becomes plain when we start walking in it. Obedience reveals truth. Obedience guarantees guidance in matters unrevealed.*

So Samuel, perhaps second-in-command to the king, came to a little town called Bethlehem, and he wanted to see the sons of Jesse. Jesse proudly paraded his seven sons before the visiting prophet. These were healthy, strapping young men, especially Eliab, who stood out among the others as Saul once did.

Read 1 Samuel 16:7, and fill in the blanks:

> But the LORD said to Samuel, "Don't judge by his _____
> or height, for I have rejected him. The LORD doesn't _____
> _____. People judge by
> outward appearance, but the LORD looks at the _____."

Isn't that a great verse—and isn't it true? We do judge by outward appearance. We size a person up based on how they look, on what we can observe. We focus so much on the outside that we often miss what's in a person's heart. We all make decisions based on the attractiveness of a person. We're hardwired that way.

This is why when Samuel saw Eliab, so tall and handsome, he thought, *This has got to be our guy.* We would have probably thought the same thing. However, God looks at the heart. This happened for each of the sons Jesse showed Samuel. The Lord said seven times, "No. Not him."

In your own words, write down the implications of the fact that people look at outward appearances and God looks at the heart. Why do you think it's important to know that God cares most about our motivations and intentions?

going backward helps us move forward.

Go Forward in Faith—Like Samuel, you can go off the last word you received from God. Stay obedient by walking in that direction until God tells you to go in a different one. God's voice will never contradict His Word, so double-check what you've felt like He's spoken to you with Scripture. If what you've received in your spirit and through the Bible line up, stay steady moving down that path.

Stand Still—Stillness can seem unproductive. However, Samuel didn't move until he was told to do so. When we pause, we often hear God's voice again, perhaps because we've been missing it as we've hurried off to one place or another. Seasons of rest are a gift. If God hasn't said, "Jump," then don't jump. Be still and know God (see Ps. 46:10). Use stillness as a time to tune in to where the Holy Spirit is guiding you.

Now read 1 Samuel 16:11–13. How do these verses describe David? What did the Lord tell Samuel to do? What changed for David "from that day on"?

The phrase "the youngest" in this context doesn't mean only that David was younger than the others. It also translates to David being his father's least favored son. Jesse was basically saying, "Yeah, I've got another son. He's a little different from his brothers. He's a musician. He plays his lyre, writes these songs to God, and watches the sheep. Frankly, I don't even want to acknowledge him."

We aren't positive why David's family treated him like an outcast, but scholars speculate that he could have been the son of a man his mother was with before she was officially married to Jesse. He was perhaps conceived "in sin" (see Ps. 51:5), making him Jesse's stepson. Or it's possible that David's mother was not the mother of Jesse's other sons. In either case, he would have not been considered a true son of Jesse and would not have had the same status as Jesse's other sons.[3] He could've also just been a little weird, and his dad and brothers didn't like it.

If you've ever felt like you were inferior or the odd one out, you can sympathize with David. Hear this: *Those who are rejected often become the chosen of the Lord.* And this is exactly how David's first steps into the narrative play out.

For him, this was a day like any other day. David was tending the sheep, and all of a sudden, a servant or one of his brothers came running. "David, they want you back in the house," this person shouted. David came, probably sweaty and smelly, bounding into the room.

God said to the prophet, "That's my boy. Anoint him." The least-favored son serving in the fields, the last choice to be considered, was God's favored and chosen one. So Samuel poured the oil on David.

What kind of person does God use? An ordinary one.
Why? So He gets the glory.

FORESHADOWING

Just as God told His prophet which new king to anoint when it came to Saul and David, so also God told many Old Testament prophets of the coming of Jesus the Messiah. Prophets such as Moses, Isaiah, Micah, Hosea, and even David himself foretold everything from the physical appearance of Jesus to His crucifixion and resurrection. Jesus' kingdom was to continue the legacy of David, be full of blessing, and endure forever.

Read the following verses, and write down prophecies about Jesus that He ultimately fulfilled. Research how many years before Jesus' birth each prophecy was given, and write down that number in your notes.

Genesis 3:15

Isaiah 7:14

Isaiah 53

Psalm 22

Micah 5:2

David was the polar opposite of Israel's first king. Saul came from a loving family, while David was disliked by his father. Saul was attractive on the outside, but inside he was vain, shallow, and devoid of true integrity. In contrast, David had a deep spiritual life and intense devotion to God. *God loves to choose ordinary people to accomplish extraordinary things.*

If God picked only the most talented, handsome, or beautiful, we'd say, "Well, of course. Look at them!" But when He picks the underqualified and overlooked, we say, "This has to be the Lord."

FORESHADOWING

Jesus also came to us in the most unexpected way. While people thought the coming Messiah would be a warrior or insurrectionist who would be born in a palace, God actually put on flesh and came as a baby born to humble parents and placed in a manger.

God didn't send the message of His coming to the religious elite or political leaders. Instead, He sent His angels to make the announcement to lowly shepherds. Jesus grew up as a carpenter's son and was fairly poor. There was nothing majestic or outstanding about His life. As He got older and entered into ministry, Jesus, like David, considered Himself a shepherd who was cast out and rejected.

Check out the following verses, and make notes of the similarities you find between Jesus' and David's lives.

Isaiah 53:3

Luke 1:26—2:40

John 10:14–16

In school, I goofed off so much in class that I once had a teacher write this on my report card: "Greg Laurie spends too much time looking out the window, daydreaming, and drawing cartoons. He will never amount to anything." Praise God that He had a different plan for my life, as He does for every life.

One of the greatest evangelists in American history was Dwight Lyman Moody, better known as D. L. Moody. To the eye, there was nothing especially noteworthy about him. However, God handpicked him while he was working in a shoe store. One of his coworkers shared the gospel with him, and Moody gave his life to Jesus Christ. He went from selling soles to saving souls, and he changed the world.[4]

In the same way, *David wasn't the obvious choice, and that made him the most obvious choice to God.*

After God chose him as the next king, what did David do? Have a parade? Put a crown on his head? No, he did something unexpected.

Pastor Chuck Swindoll wrote an excellent book on David, in which he says:

> Here's our first good look at David. He walks into the house, still smelling like sheep, and all of a sudden an old man hobbles over and pours oil on his head. It drips down his hair and drops on to his neck. Josephus, the historian, writes, "Samuel the aged whispered in his ear the meaning of the symbol, 'You will be the next king.'"
>
> What did David do? What *do* you do in a situation like that? I mean, it doesn't come along every other day. God's ways are so marvelous, aren't they? At the most surprising moment, the most magnificent things happen. "You're going to be the next king." What did he do? Well, I'm happy to report, he did not go down to the nearest department store and try on crowns. He didn't order a new set of business cards, telling the printer, "Change it from shepherd to king-elect." Didn't have a badge saying, "I'm the new man." Didn't shine up a chariot and race through the streets of Bethlehem, yelling, "I'm God's choice ... you're looking at Saul's replacement!"

What did he do?

It made no difference that Samuel had anointed him with oil. He didn't bronze that horn and hang it up in his tent. He didn't expect special treatment from others. No, he simply went back to the sheep.[5]

This is where we leave the king-to-be, back to being faithful in the field with his sheep. Sometime later, David had a déjà vu moment. He was minding his own business with the flock when he was again called for, this time by the king. Read 1 Samuel 16:14–21, and answer the following questions:

What tormented Saul?

What did Saul say to his attendants?

How did the servant answer?

BREAKING THE FOURTH WALL

God called me, David, a man after His own heart, which was a huge deal. As a shepherd, I didn't really know all this. I just saw the twinkle in Samuel's eye as he looked at my dirty face and anointed my head with oil.

Now that I've heard that phrase stated about me so often, I'm curious:

Is there someone you would identify as a man or a woman after your own heart? How do you feel about them? What do you think that means about how God felt toward me?

It was kind of strange to be anointed in such an outstanding way and then just go back to my high school job. You may have worked at a restaurant or clothing store as a teenager. I tended sheep. Samuel was old, and some days out in the field I thought maybe he had just officially lost his marbles. I couldn't be a king. I was an outcast.

When the messengers arrived at the house of Jesse, what did he do?

How did Saul feel about David?

David stepped out of the field and into the palace, not as a king but as a musician and servant. Why? As I've heard said before, "If serving is below you, leadership is beyond you."[6] Before we can take a public platform, God may have us sit with our calling and allow Him to work with us in the secret place.

Take a moment to write down the secret places God has set you in. How do you think God sees you there?

With David, anytime his public platform exceeded the strength of his foundation in God, his life crumbled (as we will see in the lessons to come). The same goes for us all. Without Christ as our firm foundation, we simply cannot withstand the weight of leadership.

How could everyone's last pick be the first in line for the throne of Israel?

Have you ever felt like the odd person out? What does it mean to you that those the world rejects God often chooses?

When the king's messenger showed up at my house, I thought he had to be there for one of my brothers who served in Saul's army. Imagine my surprise when Dad summoned me from the field and told me about playing my music for the king. Then, not that long later, as he packed my bag and sent me on my way, it seemed as if everything was about to change. Maybe Samuel had been right after all. But I wasn't headed to the palace to rule—God placed me there to serve.

Why do you think God calls us into secret places to serve before we lead?

David's Diary

Slowly and reflectively read the following psalm aloud.

Psalm 4

Answer me when I call to you,
   O God who declares me innocent.
Free me from my troubles.
   Have mercy on me and hear my prayer.

How long will you people ruin my reputation?
   How long will you make groundless accusations?
   How long will you continue your lies?
You can be sure of this:
   The LORD set apart the godly for himself.
   The LORD will answer when I call to him.

Don't sin by letting anger control you.
   Think about it overnight and remain silent.
Offer sacrifices in the right spirit,
   and trust the LORD.

Many people say, "Who will show us better times?"
   Let your face smile on us, LORD.
You have given me greater joy
   than those who have abundant harvests of grain and new wine.
In peace I will lie down and sleep,
   for you alone, O LORD, will keep me safe.

Think deeply about what you just read. Use all your senses, emotions, and imagination to interact with this psalm. Feel free to underline words or doodle or write.

Respond to all you've received. Take a moment to compile your thoughts and turn them into a prayer to God. I will start you with a short prayer, and then you can use the rest of the space to run with your own. You can pray out loud, with others, or silently in your heart.

Father, thank You for David's life and story. We're so grateful for how it ultimately points to the way Jesus has chosen all of us for the extraordinary purpose of serving Him. We thank You that You saw David being faithful to the field work You called him to, and we ask that You instill the same faithfulness in us to follow You. May we, too, become people after Your heart.

In Jesus' name, amen.

Personal Psalm Writing

Following David's "I'm-struggling-and-yet-I-trust" pattern, use the space on this page and in other Personal Psalm Writing sections to write your own psalm based on your current situation and prayers. Get creative! Everyone has their own style. Use the psalms in this study as a template, or design your own. If you need a starting point, here's a writing formula you can follow:

- Title
- Description of your pain, complaint, or struggle
- Reminder of who God is and what He can do
- Declaration of how you are believing God is still trustworthy

HOW TO OVERCOME YOUR GIANTS

*Am I the only one in this camp who remembers
the greatness of God, who this beast has defied?*

DAVID, SEASON 1, EPISODE 8, HOUSE OF DAVID

*You come to me with sword, spear, and
javelin, but I come to you in the name of the
LORD of Heaven's Armies—the God of the
armies of Israel, whom you have defied.*

1 SAMUEL 17:45

WE ALL HAVE GIANTS

All of us face giants in life: problems that seem insurmountable or a secret sin we try to conquer but that seems only to loom larger with the passing of time. You may have already overcome giants, like quitting an addiction or setting the goal to share the gospel with someone who intimidates you. Possibly you're standing up to a giant right now.

In those moments when we're face to face with an issue that has tripped us up time and time again—a fear that keeps us up at night, a threat that taunts us day in and day out, or a family member we keep praying for but never see an answer about—it's easy to begin to believe our giant is unstoppable.

When we boil it down, a giant is anyone or anything that seeks to control, hurt, destroy, or torment us in life.

Take a moment to identify any giants you are up against in these areas of your life:

AREAS	GIANTS
Relational	
Mental	
Spiritual	
Physical	
Emotional	
Other	

DIRECTOR'S CUT: A BRIEF HISTORY ABOUT GIANTS ACCORDING TO THE BIBLE

I know, giants feel like something we made up for fairy tales and fantasy fiction. However, according to the Bible, they were completely real. They may not have chased Jack down a beanstalk shouting, "Fee-fi-fo-fum," but they were extremely large, powerful, and intimidating.

Goliath emerged from a clan of giant men called the Anakim (or Anakites), who were the descendants of the giant Anak (see Num. 13:28, 32–33; Deut. 2:11). They resided in the southern section of the land of Canaan in Joshua 15:13. Other giant groups mentioned in the Bible are the Emim (or Emites) and the Zamzummim (or Zamzummites; see Deut. 2:10–11, 20).[1] The largest

man in recent history was Robert Wadlow, who reached the towering height of 8 feet, 11 inches tall. He was affectionately known as the "gentle giant."[2] Goliath had at least a foot on old Robert, but he certainly was not known as gentle.

Amos 2:9–10 gives us a figurative depiction of Amorite giants, describing them as being "as tall

How do we overcome our giants?

To get our answer, we're going to look at the very familiar story of David and Goliath. If you grew up in church, you've probably heard this story since childhood. As a result, the account can become like a fairy tale. However, this teenage shepherd boy standing up to a giant of a man in the middle of a war zone was a historical event, and his story applies to the reality of our own lives today when it comes to overcoming fears, obstacles, and hardships.

Do you remember where we left our soon-to-be king? David was spending time in King Saul's palace playing a lyre to drive the dark spirits from him. But later David was sent home, and he went back to tending sheep in the field. While David was going back and forth between playing his music and working on the family ranch, a new conflict was developing between the Israelites and their longtime enemy, the Philistines. Tensions finally boiled into a battle between the two armies, in the Valley of Elah.

Imagine it: On one slope was the Philistine army, on the other slope were the Israelites, and in the middle stood a hulk of a Philistine warrior named Goliath. He was approximately nine feet, six inches of solid muscle covered in body armor, and he came out every day to taunt not only the Israelite army but also their God.

GOLIATH
giant man
Philistine warrior
arrogant

Take a look at 1 Samuel 17:8–11, and answer the following questions:

What did the Philistine giant ask for Saul's men to do?

as cedars and as strong as oaks." Joshua and Caleb, when they observed the giants in the land of Canaan, reported back to Moses: "All the people we saw were huge" (Num. 13:32). Goliath's height is described in 1 Samuel 17:4 as "over nine feet tall," or about three meters tall.

The Bible mentions the Israelites conquering several other giants as well, such as Og (Ps. 135:11), Ishbi-benob (2 Sam. 21:16), Saph (2 Sam. 21:18), and Goliath's brother, Lahmi (1 Chron. 20:5). Scholars believe these stories were considered important enough to place into the Scriptures because they were historical examples of how the

Israelites overcame impossible circumstances through God's strength.[3] Their God was always greater, and nothing—not even the greatest of giants—could stand against Him.

What was the deal that Goliath wanted to make?

How did the Israelites react to the giant's words?

No one was exactly competing for the chance to jump into the ring with Goliath. There was a lot riding on this battle, for one thing. On top of that, going up against a giant seemed like choosing certain death. Out of everyone on that hillside, King Saul—with his great height, strong build, and royal armor—would have been the most likely candidate. However, even he stayed glued to his spot.

This stalemate went on for forty days. Some of David's brothers were in the army. Eventually, Jesse got itchy and wanted some news, so he decided that his sons at the battle probably needed a snack. He summoned David out of the field (again!) to make an Uber Eats delivery to the front lines of battle, not knowing his least-favored son was about to deliver so much more.

Read 1 Samuel 17:20–24, 32, and fill in the blanks:

> So David left the sheep with another shepherd and set out _____
> _____, as Jesse had directed him. He arrived at the camp just
> as _____ with
> shouts and battle cries. Soon the Israelite and Philistine forces stood facing each
> other, army against army. David left his things with the keeper of supplies and hur-
> ried out to _____ to greet his brothers.
> As he was talking with them, Goliath, the Philistine champion from Gath, came
> out from the Philistine ranks. Then David _____
> _____ to the army of Israel.
> As soon as the Israelite army saw him, they began to run away in fright....
> "Don't worry about this Philistine," David told Saul. "I'll go _____
> _____!"

David was a courageous young man. He had killed lions and bears to protect his sheep. He wanted to go down and face off with Goliath because, in his eyes, *Goliath was big, but God was bigger.*

He had been rescued before, and he knew he'd be rescued again. So, after convincing Saul to let him go into battle, David did yet another unthinkable thing: he rejected Saul's offer to wear his armor. It was just too loose and awkward on his adolescent body.

He walked in his everyday garb down to the stream in the middle of the valley and gathered five smooth stones from the water. He carefully placed the rocks in his shepherd's bag, readied his sling in his hand, and advanced toward the Philistine. In response to the giant's taunting and cursing, David gave the strongest pregame speech in history:

> "You come to me with sword, spear, and javelin, but I come to you in the name of the LORD of Heaven's Armies—the God of the armies of Israel, whom you have defied. Today the LORD will conquer you, and I will kill you and cut off your head. And then I will give the dead bodies of your men to the birds and wild animals, and the whole world will know that there is a God in Israel! And everyone assembled here will know that the LORD rescues his people, but not with sword or spear. This is the LORD's battle, and he will give you to us!"
>
> As Goliath moved closer to attack, David quickly ran out to meet him. Reaching into his shepherd's bag and taking out a stone, he hurled it with his sling and hit the Philistine in the forehead. The stone sank in, and Goliath stumbled and fell face down on the ground.
>
> So David triumphed over the Philistine with only a sling and a stone, for he had no sword. Then David ran over and pulled Goliath's sword from its sheath. David used it to kill him and cut off his head.
>
> When the Philistines saw that their champion was dead, they turned and ran. Then the men of Israel and Judah gave a great a shout of triumph and rushed after the Philistines, chasing them as far as Gath and the gates of Ekron. The bodies of the dead and wounded Philistines were strewn all along the road from Shaaraim, as far as Gath and Ekron. Then the Israelite army returned and plundered the deserted Philistine camp. (1 Sam. 17:45–53)

Looking at the highlighted areas, what stands out to you most? Why?

BREAKING THE FOURTH WALL

Can you believe I slayed a giant? Sometimes I still can't fathom I did either. My heart had never beat that fast, and my feet had never sprinted so swiftly in my young life. I believed in God and, wouldn't ya know it, He came through for me. To Him be the glory! There's so much that happened on that fateful day when I defeated Goliath and the Israelites were empowered to claim their victory.

As you read this story, what stood out to you? Did you learn anything new?

I clearly remember putting on Saul's armor and just how heavy and awkward it felt. I even felt a bit embarrassed, not to mention completely immobilized. I knew if I ran out to meet Goliath in that, I'd certainly die. So, I took it off.

It seemed brave, I know, to run out there in just my dirty tunic, but really it was the only thing I felt confident in. God had trained me against the lion and the bear in that garb and with my simple sling. So, I trusted in the lessons and weapons He had gifted me, and I trusted Him to lead us to victory. Now, knowing my battle strategy, what can you apply from my actions to your own life?

Everyone loves a good Cinderella story, especially one in which the underdog takes the win, and David beating Goliath is the pinnacle of the genre. David had the odds stacked against him. He was no one's first draft pick. However, he placed the battle in God's hands and received the victory.

What do we learn from this about defeating our own giants? We probably won't ever have to fight a massive bodybuilder in a war. However, we all will face hardships, seemingly insurmountable obstacles, and what seem like irresistible temptations.

Read 1 Corinthians 10:13. What does it say about temptation? What will God always provide for us when we are tempted?

While it is true that we all have giants, it is also true that every giant is defeatable.

THE BATTLE BELONGS TO THE LORD

The most important fact we need to know in order to defeat our giants is that the battle belongs to the Lord. If we try to conquer giants in our own might, we will fail. Like David clanging and clunking along in Saul's armor, we'd be swinging swords we're not strong enough to carry at an enemy we are not equipped to fight. The truth of the matter is that giants are really big and powerful. While they are much larger than us, they are not greater than our God.

Most giants don't start out big. It's weird to think about, but Goliath was once a baby. What mother looks at her child and thinks, *Oh, what a sweet boy! I'll name him Goliath*? Maybe they had a nickname for him like "Olly" that seemed a little more befitting an infant. In any case, he was once small. Then, he grew, ate steaks, did a few bench presses, and became a warrior. I'm sure everyone ran for cover when it came time to change his diaper.

The same goes for our own problems: they started out as small issues, didn't they?

The financial struggle started out as a few dollars overspent. The addiction began as one drink or hit. The marriage began unraveling because of a fleeting feeling of resentment. Those lustful thoughts became more frequent, giving way to actions you deeply regretted. The panic attacks now were sparked years ago with that first anxious thought. The hopeless fear that our loved one will never come to know Jesus started sinking in when we noticed our prayers were going unanswered.

Our problems and sins can grow from one small issue into towering giants that threaten to bring us down, and this puts us right into the shoes of David standing before Goliath as the giant taunts and jeers. Look at the following verse, and note David's response.

1 Samuel 17:47

FORESHADOWING

In the same way that David showed up to fight Goliath, Jesus is our champion. He ran before us to take on the consequences of our sin, the Devil, and the grave, and He defeated them once and for all. On the day He was crucified, Jesus conquered evil and gave victory to His people forever.

Look up the following verses, and note any similarities between Jesus' and David's battle strategies:

Hebrews 2:10

John 3:16–17

1 John 3:8

I'm sure if David had been given the option, he would have shrunk Goliath to a less intimidating size. But he didn't have that option, and we don't either. Our giants are full-grown, and we have to face them. As we do, it's key that we understand, as David did, that this fight isn't ours. The battle is the Lord's.

It's interesting that David so strongly understood this and yet didn't discount that God could use him in the fight. He still allowed God to place him face to face with Goliath and use his talents to defeat the giant.

Props

©jgroup/iStock/Getty Images Plus

David was skilled with a sling and used it as a mighty weapon. Shepherds commonly carried slings to defend themselves and their sheep from predators. Slings were also deadly weapons in ancient armies, just as important as bows and arrows or swords. As an experienced slinger from his time in the field, David would have loaded the strip of leather or fabric with a rock, spun it with great force, and hurled it at his target at as much as one hundred miles per hour, making the nearly invisible projectile lethal.[4]

So if God has called you to face a giant, chances are He's also equipped you for the fight. He's on your side in the battle and has gifted you many spiritual weapons, plus He will offer others during the fight itself.

Read through this list of weapons, and write out the verse each one is found in.

Weapon	Reference	Verse
Sword of the Spirit (the Word of God)	Ephesians 6:17	
Prayer	Ephesians 6:18	
Praise and worship	2 Chronicles 20:20	
Name of Jesus	Philippians 2:9–11	
Shield of faith	Ephesians 6:16	
Your testimony	Acts 1:8	
Your testimony	Revelation 12:11	

On top of our spiritual battle arsenal, we also have access to all the unique skills we've developed over the span of our lives. We may not be professional stone throwers, but we might be great party hosts, office workers, parents, friends, musicians, mathematicians, networkers, athletes, communicators, or something else.

Use the space below to jot down a few of your unique weapons.

Take a look at what God trained you with in the field, and ask Him how He could help you use it to take your giant down. And don't be afraid to get creative. David was expected to use armor and a sword but chose a sling instead. Don't be afraid to trust in the skills God has developed in you, even if they aren't the most obvious choice for your battle.

CLOSE-UP

I know it seems like we're reading a fairy tale when we talk about facing a giant. But literal giants were real! Though they no longer roam the earth, we do face life battles and seemingly insurmountable situational struggles that we could classify as giant problems. As you pause to observe some of your giants and take in the full size of them, think back to the first time you encountered them.

How did the giants in your life start out? What did the issues you are up against now look like when they were small? How do they look now that they're big?

As if the Holy Spirit were whispering in his ear, David knew in his heart that he had to take down Goliath with a rock and sling. Sure, there were other weapons available to him on that battlefield. However, he wasn't trained with them. He wasn't a warrior (yet); he was a shepherd boy. A sling was what he had in his hand.

Let's take a moment to figure out what God has placed in your hand to fight your battle.

Which spiritual weapons stand out to you the most from the list in this lesson?

Why do you think they would be effective against your giant?

Have you been discounting your own skill set in the fight?

How has God uniquely equipped you for battle?

ATTACK YOUR GIANTS

Earlier in the story, we read that the Israelites had been asking, "Have you seen the giant?... He comes out each day to defy Israel'" (1 Sam. 17:25). In other words, Goliath wasn't just down in the valley. He had climbed up and was walking through the camp of Israel taunting the army. "Hey, hey, who wants to fight me? Come on. Who is man enough?" He was right up in their faces and wasn't going away.

That's how it is with giants. You compromise here, you compromise there, and now they've invaded your life. They're seemingly everywhere and becoming even more powerful. So what do you do?

When it comes to these sins, you don't run from giants, negotiate with them, or yell at them. You attack them. (Remember, we're talking about spiritual enemies here.) You don't say, "I'll get to this one day." You deal with your giant *right now*.

Look at 1 Samuel 17:48. What direction did David run?

He didn't run from Goliath. He didn't just hold his ground either. He attacked! We must do the same. Whatever problem we're facing, we need to stop hiding from it and making excuses for it. We have to face it and finish the sin giant off. We can't give it a second chance at taking over our lives.

Then, after Goliath was down on the ground, David did something that sort of anticipated modern filmmaking. You know that moment when the hero thinks he has defeated the villain and turns his back to walk away and the bad guy jumps back up and attacks him from behind? Viewers see the villain coming, and they want to scream, "Turn around! He's not dead! Kill the villain before he kills you!" David must've had a hunch such a thing might happen.

Have you ever watched a scene like this play out in a movie? If so, what happened?

David was not about to let that happen. He was not going to give this giant a second chance. So what did he do? Read 1 Samuel 17:51, and write down what David did to officially defeat Goliath:

If we don't defeat our sin giants, they will defeat us. It's our choice. Destroy them. Don't apologize for them. Don't allow a giant to keep living by rationalizing, making excuses, or misnaming sin by calling it a "mistake," "human weakness," or "a lapse in judgment." *Call sin "sin," and then finish it off.*

David did this later in his life after he made a huge mistake by claiming a married woman for himself (we'll unpack this more later). As he was wrestling with the weight of what he'd done, he wrote Psalm 51. Read this Scripture, and fill in the blanks:

Have mercy on me, O God,
  because of your

_____.

Because of your

_____,

  blot out the stain of my sins.
Wash me clean from my

_____.

Purify me from my _____.
  (vv. 1–2)

Now let's look up 1 John 1:9 and answer the following questions:

In your own words, what does *confess* mean?

What is God's response when we confess our sins?

The Greek word behind *confess* in this verse simply means to acknowledge and agree with God.[5] Here's an example: If you and I were standing on the beach watching a beautiful sunset, and I said, "That is beautiful," you might say, "I agree." In the same way, when we align ourselves with God's view of the world, and He says about

BREAKING THE FOURTH WALL

I'm not going to lie: Goliath's sword was heavy as I lifted it out of the sheath. It was hard to hold not only because of its size but also because of the weight of the situation. I had killed animals while protecting sheep, but now I was going to cut off a giant's head. It sounds gory, and, truthfully, it was. However, the alternative was to let him wake up and come back for another fight. I had to decide to defeat God's enemy once and for all. So I grabbed that sword and swung with all my adolescent strength. (I was pretty fit from all the time I spent herding sheep and doing labor around the farm, if I do say so myself.) I have to admit, it took a few good whacks to complete the task.

Sometimes we don't want to finish off our giants, though. It's hard work, isn't it? There's some heavy lifting involved. Let these questions help you start to lift your sword high to finish your fight.

Does your giant have a name? Is there a sin struggle you've been dealing with? What is it? Call it out and bring it into the light.

Have you been allowing your giant to live by misnaming it or apologizing for it rather than repenting and getting rid of it?

What do you think it would take for you to come into alignment with God's will and allow Him to move on your behalf to help you give your sin giant a death blow?

His ways, "This is wonderful—I love it," we must say, "I agree. I love it too, Lord." When God looks at sin and says, "This breaks my heart—I hate it," our response must be, "It breaks my heart too, God. I'm so sorry."

By calling out our giant, our sin, we are agreeing with God about the darkness and bringing it into the light. We are running toward it, ready to give it a metaphorical death blow, becoming overcomers in Christ and allowing God to have to the final word of victory over every situation and sin.

SUIT UP (OR DOWN)

In 1 Samuel 17:38, mere minutes before David went down to face Goliath, King Saul said something similar to, "Well, you need to wear some armor, boy. I'll tell you what—you can wear mine." So David put on a bronze helmet and a coat of mail, and he strapped on Saul's sword. He took a step or two to see what it was like, because he was just a shepherd and a kid who had never worn armor before. Then he said, "I can't go in these," and stripped it all off (v. 39). He was not going to wear Saul's armor. It was going to be God or nothing.

The problem with our human perspectives is that we tend to believe that Satan is the giant and God is small when the opposite is true. Satan is powerful, but God is more powerful. *We don't need to learn to suit up and become a hero; we need to see Jesus operating as the greater David on our behalf.*

Remember the agreement that Goliath initially made with the Israelites? He said, "Choose one man to come down here and fight me! If he kills me, then we will be your slaves. But if I kill him, you will be our slaves!" (1 Sam. 17:8–9). Because David won, the entire Israelite army shared in his victory. As a result, they found the courage to attack the Philistines, courage they had lacked before.

BREAKING THE FOURTH WALL

Now, I was a pretty excellent marksman with my sling. But I have to give God all the praise for nailing Goliath. What if the wind had been blowing differently that day? What if I had tripped over a divot in the ground while I was running toward Goliath? What if my sling had broken?

There were a million factors in play for me to nail Goliath just right and bring him down. It's clear not only that I fought for God but, more importantly, that He fought for me and for all of Israel. This makes me wonder:

What does it look like for you to allow Jesus, the greater David, to fight on your behalf?

Have you been fighting your battles in your own power or by relying on Christ? Have you tried on someone

FORESHADOWING

In the same way that the Israelites won when David defeated Goliath, Jesus Christ went to the cross and defeated death, sin, and Satan on our behalf. We, too, share in His victory.

Look up 1 John 5:4–5, and fill in the blanks:

For every child of God _____ this evil world, and we achieve this _____ through our faith. And who can win this _____ against the world? Only those who believe that _____.

David's actions emboldened the Israelite army. How would you say that Christ as the greater David also gives us courage to finish our fight?

Therefore, we don't fight for *victory. We don't have to go take on our giants in our own strength. We fight* from *our victory in Christ, knowing He's already won the battle.*

I will fail. You will fail. Satan is way more powerful than Greg. He's way more powerful than you. However, the Lord is so much stronger than Satan. So stand on the power of the Lord's might. Allow it to give you the boldness and strength to do what God has called you to do. Just as the

else's armor (their advice or nonbiblical "truth") and realized that it just didn't work for you? What was the outcome?

Yes, I made a bold choice to step out and face Goliath. But it had to be done. I know it takes courage, so as you step out, I'm cheering you on.

What have you been doing when it comes to your giants—fighting or hiding? What do you want to choose?

How does the knowledge that we can fight *from the victory* we already have in Jesus instead of *for it* give you greater courage when it comes to life's battles?

Israelites shared in the victory of David, be assured that we, too, ultimately share in the victory of Christ. Let that truth empower you to move forward and fight your battle.

Like David, we all have a choice to make when a giant invades the valleys of our lives. Will we step out to fight in faith or hide and allow the giant to taunt us and take over our lives?

In the following chart, contrast the lies our giants tell us with the truth of God's Word. In the left column, write down what lies you're tempted to believe. In the right column, write down a Scripture to help you see the victory God offers you in that area.

Use the concordance in the back of your Bible to find verses by looking up words describing what you're struggling with, such as *anxiety*, *identity*, or *money*. For each topic there will be Scriptures that point to God's truths in these areas. See the example to get started.

LIE	TRUTH
I need to worry about my future.	Look at the birds. They don't plant or harvest or store food in barns, for your heavenly Father feeds them. And aren't you far more valuable to him than they are? (Matt. 6:26).

As lies that the Enemy has taunted you with resurface in your mind, come back to this list and defeat them with "the sword of the Spirit, which is the word of God" (Eph. 6:17). Claiming victory in Jesus through Scripture is how we begin to put on our armor and step into the fight full of faith.

If we truly want to take out our giants, we have to have a relationship with Christ, and we must allow His power to move in and through us to set ourselves and others free.

David's Diary

Slowly and reflectively read the following psalm aloud.

Psalm 16

Keep me safe, O God,
 for I have come to you for refuge.

I said to the LORD, "You are my Master!
 Every good thing I have comes from you."
The godly people in the land
 are my true heroes!
 I take pleasure in them!
Troubles multiply for those who chase after other gods.
 I will not take part in their sacrifices of blood
 or even speak the names of their gods.

LORD, you alone are my inheritance, my cup of blessing.
 You guard all that is mine.
The land you have given me is a pleasant land.
 What a wonderful inheritance!

I will bless the LORD who guides me;
 even at night my heart instructs me.
I know the LORD is always with me.
 I will not be shaken, for he is right beside me.

No wonder my heart is glad, and I rejoice.
 My body rests in safety.
For you will not leave my soul among the dead
 or allow your holy one to rot in the grave.
You will show me the way of life,
 granting me the joy of your presence
 and the pleasures of living with you forever.

Think deeply about what you just read. Use all your senses, emotions, and imagination to interact with this psalm. Feel free to underline words or doodle or write.

Respond to all you've received. Take a moment to compile your thoughts and turn them into a prayer. I will start you off, and then you can use the rest of the space to continue with your own. You can pray out loud or silently, with a group or by yourself.

> *Jesus, I need You. I need my sin forgiven. I've been fighting on my own to change my life and pull myself up by my bootstraps, but I keep failing. The battle is too much for me. I've tried to fill the hole in my heart with so many things that culture has offered and realize that nothing satisfies. I need help. I need You, God.*
>
> *Lord Jesus, I'm not going to make excuses anymore. I know I'm a sinner. I also now know that You're the Savior who died on the cross for my sin and rose again from the dead. I turn from my sin now, and I choose to follow You from this moment forward. Thank You for offering me freedom and victory in Jesus.*

> *In Jesus' name I pray, amen.*

Personal Psalm Writing

Following David's "I'm-struggling-and-yet-I-trust" pattern, use the space on this page and in other Personal Psalm Writing sections to write your own psalm based on your current situation and prayers. If you're having a hard time getting started, see the end of lesson 1 for ideas of how you can compose your own psalm.

WHAT TO DO WHEN THINGS FALL APART

Fear is the enemy. Fear is the thief.

DAVID, SEASON 1, EPISODE 1, HOUSE OF DAVID

Then I pray to you, O LORD. I say, "You are my place of refuge. You are all I really want in life."

PSALM 142:5

MOVE FROM COWARDLY TO COURAGEOUS

David reminds me of legendary singer-songwriter Johnny Cash—mainly because they were both flawed people. Now, the Bible is filled with people with deficiencies. The only one who is perfect is Jesus, right? However, there are certain characters in the Bible whose sin is never mentioned (though it was surely there). Examples include Joseph and several of the prophets.

David was not one of them. Did you know there is more biblical content dedicated to David than to any other biblical character outside of Jesus?[1] While we learn a lot about David's victories, we learn just as much about his failures and sins. Even so, Scripture describes David as a man after God's own heart (see 1 Sam. 13:14).

Like David, Johnny Cash had his doubts and disappointments. One event that deeply shaped Johnny's life was the tragic death of his older brother, Jack. Jack and Johnny were inseparable. Johnny really looked up to his older brother. Jack wanted to be a preacher one day; Johnny, a singer. But Jack, while a teenager, thought he should take an extra job to make a little money for the family because they were very poor. He was working at a sawmill and somehow got pulled into the saw. It was a horrible accident that affected Johnny for the rest of his life.

Johnny and Jack's father, Ray, could be a very cold man. He actually said in the presence of Johnny, "The wrong son died."[2] Imagine going through life with a statement like that hanging over your head. Johnny spent the rest of his life trying to win the approval of his dad and pouring his pain into his songs.

In some ways, Johnny was like a modern-day psalmist. He reminds me of David because David, too, was unloved by his father and poured out his own heart and pain into his poetry and music. While we don't know if David ever lost a brother, we do know he was a chosen king waiting to take the throne of Saul, and this created tension between these great men.

To fully understand David's story, there are a few things we need to know about his predecessor, Saul.

Saul had some fine qualities that our culture values today, such as fame, followers, power, and wealth. He was really handsome. If he were alive today, he would be an influencer on social media and would probably be elected to office if he ran. In short, he had it all going on. But Saul sinned against God and did not repent, so he was disqualified from being king.

The house of Saul was built around glorifying himself, while the house of David had its foundations set on bringing God glory. Around 1 Samuel 13 is when things really start to go south for Saul. Here are a few of the coinciding events:

- Samuel instructed Saul to wait to make a sacrifice to God before his battle against the Philistines. Saul and his men got tired of waiting, and he decided to make the sacrifice before Samuel's arrival (13:9).
- Samuel told Saul that because of his decision, he had lost his kingdom and God had chosen his successor, "a man after [God's] own heart" (13:14).
- Saul chose to dismiss Samuel and surround himself instead with poor influences like Ahijah, the grandson of an unfaithful priest (14:3).
- Jonathan, Saul's son, sneaked into the opposing camp without telling his father. Because of Jonathan's faith, God sent the Philistines into a panic, and the ground shook. God gave Israel the victory (14:23).

- Saul assembled his men and threw them into the battle. Due to his making rash leadership decisions without consulting the Lord, his men sinned against God when they finally got to eat (14:33).
- Saul tried to pray to God, but because of his disobedience, God didn't answer him that day (14:37).
- Instead of owning his mistakes, Saul tried to blame God's silence on Jonathan and threatened to kill him. The men who had witnessed Jonathan in battle testified on his behalf and saved his life (14:44–45).
- Saul again didn't carry out God's instructions in a battle against the Amalekites (15:9).
- Saul set up a monument in his own honor and tried to defend himself when confronted by Samuel, stating that he did carry out the Lord's instructions (15:12–21).
- Samuel told Saul that he had been rejected as king because he had rejected God. As Samuel left, Saul grabbed Samuel's robe and tore it. Samuel used this as an illustration to show that the kingdom of Israel had been torn from Saul and given to someone better than him (15:26–29).

All these events in Saul's life set the stage for David to step into his calling. After this, Samuel anointed David to become king, and he entered Saul's service to soothe him with music. (After God removed His hand from Saul, an evil spirit would often torment him, but David's music would bring him some comfort.) Shortly after, David stepped onto the battlefield and defeated Goliath.

While things were looking up for David, Saul was down because he knew his time as a ruler was coming to an end. As a result, Saul became afraid of David. He saw David no longer as his faithful musician but as a threat, and he turned on David.

FORESHADOWING

Jesus, too, was anointed and abandoned. He declared His purpose in the synagogue and was enabled, as God in flesh, to perform miraculous works that further proved He was the long-awaited Messiah. The Pharisees, a group of religious leaders at the time, saw that Jesus was undermining their authority, so they were continuously trying to devise a plan to murder Him. When their scheming finally led to Jesus' arrest, His own disciples left him to His captors.

Review the following verses, and note any correlations you find between David's and Jesus' journeys from being anointed to abandoned.

Luke 4:18–19

Acts 10:38

John 12:3

Matthew 12:14

Mark 15:34

Matthew 26:56

Then there was that song written by the young women of Israel ...

This was their song:

> "Saul has killed his thousands,
>   and David his ten thousands!"

This made Saul very angry. "What's this?" he said. "They credit David with ten thousands and me with only thousands. Next they'll be making him their king!" So from that time on Saul kept a jealous eye on David. (1 Sam. 18:7–9)

Open your Bible to 1 Samuel 18:7–16, and answer the following questions:

What did Saul throw at David? Why?

What did Saul give David command over?

David was *what* "in everything he did"?

Why was David always successful?

Why do you think Saul was afraid of David?

Saul was afraid of David, but David was also afraid of Saul. Up until this point, we've seen David only as a brave young man. He had been faithful in defending his sheep, he was a giant-killer in the Valley of Elah, and he boldly stepped into the king's court with his Stratocaster electric guitar to play some amazingly sweet riffs that consoled Saul. He'd been a champ. However, suddenly cowardice replaced David's courage.

Fear is a powerful emotion, isn't it? When it grips us in life, it can take us over and warp how we see everything. I once heard *fear* defined with the acronym FEAR:

F—False
E—Evidence
A—Appearing
R—Real

When we copy things down, we commit them to memory. So take a moment to copy down the acronym for yourself.

F—
E—
A—
R—

This is exactly what was happening to both David and Saul. Saul threw a spear at David. His life was in danger. We get why David was afraid and on the run. But why was Saul afraid of David? Because David was a threat to his power and position.

We have all experienced this in some way, because people like power. We can get angry and jealous when someone else gets the raise, promotion, or opportunity. We don't like it when people get something we think we deserve. This type of fear can cause even the best of friends to turn on each other. People have been known to lie, blame, or undermine others to bring them down in order to stay on top.

Have you experienced fear that caused a fallout in a situation or relationship? What happened? What role do you think that fear played in this scenario?

Fear is ugly and can ruin our lives. Saul accurately summed up fear's effects on his own choices when he stated, "Yes, I have sinned. I have disobeyed your instructions and the LORD's command, for I was afraid of the people and did what they demanded" (1 Sam. 15:24).

While David, too, made many mistakes throughout his life, he allowed his faith to trump his fear. We see this in his writing. Read Psalm 51:10, and fill in the blanks:

Create in me a _____ heart, O God.
Renew a _____ within me.

David's belief in God ultimately guided his decisions. From him we learn that *the choice to operate out of courage instead of cowardice makes all the difference.*

THOUGH PEOPLE ABANDON US, GOD NEVER WILL

At this point in his life, that field of sheep was probably looking pretty good to David. At least there, he knew who his enemies were. A bear or a lion was clearly a predator out for his sheep. But now David had been promoted in Saul's court. He was leading armies into battle. He had stepped into the world of political intrigue and had to figure out who his true friends and foes were.

Sometimes his enemies were surprisingly nearby. While it was clear that David's dad and brothers didn't favor him and that Saul was becoming his enemy, he probably didn't suspect that his own wife would turn on him.

Saul devised a plan to rid himself of David by telling him he could marry a princess—Saul's daughter—if he killed one hundred Philistines. Saul figured there was no way David could do this. The Philistines would kill him and solve a big problem for Saul. (David himself later used this

BREAKING THE FOURTH WALL

Sheer shock bolted through my body when Saul threw that spear at me. There I was, just playing my lyre, and *wham!* Good thing I was quick on my feet because I had to dodge Saul twice.

The fact that Saul tried to kill me while he was having one of his manic episodes was wild, but what struck me the deepest was the fear I saw behind the madness in his eyes. I was

a shepherd boy and musician turned warrior but still a mere servant in the house of Saul. Yet I could sense just how afraid of me Saul truly was.

I had no plans to overthrow his throne in some kind of military coup. I wouldn't have even thought of planning to murder him. Everything was in the hands of God. Instead of having a heart-to-heart with me to understand how I felt, Saul operated out of fear.

I've felt that way before, though. Haven't you? We've all tried to prevent something from occurring because we're scared of the unknown. Anxieties can drive us into fight-or-flight mode when really we should lean into the present moment in faith. Do you know what I mean?

Is there an area in your life where you're operating more out of fear

strategy to get rid of Uriah; maybe he learned it here.) But David, being the warrior that he was, gathered his men and killed not one hundred but *two hundred Philistines!*

I can imagine Saul's shock as David made good on his promise. Saul had no choice then but to offer David his daughter Michal.

Saul was bothered even more when he realized that Michal had actually come to love her new husband. How his plan had backfired! Worse, David continued to meet success in battle. The people loved him more and more, and this drove Saul to destruction. He finally decided to take matters into his own hands.

Read 1 Samuel 19:11–18, and answer the following questions:

MICHAL
David's first wife
caught up in family politics
loved & despised David

What did Michal warn David about?

How did David escape?

What excuse did Michal give to the men on David's behalf?

than faith? Can you identify what you are afraid of and why?

I found it strange that Saul swung from wanting me dead to offering me a position as a commander, leading at least a thousand men. Though Saul acted out of fear, I knew God wanted me to be brave.

He offered me the position, and I stepped up into it.

What would it look like for you to shift your focus so you could start making decisions based on courage instead of cowardice?

We're not even halfway through my story, but let's pause for a moment and take note of what we've learned so far by answering this question: What does comparing my legacy to Saul's teach you about fear and faith?

What did Michal tell her father that David had said?

Where did David go when he fled? Whom did he find?

Initially, Michal was on David's side. She warned him of her father's plot. But in the end, she covered for herself and threw David under the bus, causing Saul's fear to erupt. In Saul's mind, he had to without a doubt destroy David. Thinking David had threatened his daughter would have only fed the flames of Saul's fears. He had a grudge he wouldn't let go of.

JONATHAN
David's best friend
son & heir of King Saul
loyal to God and David

Just when it seemed things couldn't get much worse for David, he was forced away from his best friend: Saul's son, Jonathan. Jonathan was the only friend David had in the whole world. He never turned on David like everyone else did. Jonathan worked behind the scenes trying to get his dad, Saul, to chill out. But eventually he realized there was nothing he could do.

So Jonathan made a solemn pact with David, saying, "May the LORD destroy all your enemies!" And Jonathan made David reaffirm his vow of friendship again, for Jonathan loved David as he loved himself.

Then Jonathan said, "Tomorrow we celebrate the new moon festival. You will be missed when your place at the table is empty. The day after tomorrow, toward evening, go to the place where you hid before, and wait there by the stone pile. I will come out and shoot three arrows to the side of the stone pile as though I were shooting at a target. Then I will send a boy to bring the arrows back. If you hear me tell him, 'They're on this side,' then you will know, as surely as the LORD lives, that all is well, and there is no trouble. But if I tell him, 'Go farther—the arrows are still ahead of you,' then it will mean that you must leave immediately, for the LORD is sending you away. And may the LORD make us keep our promises to each other, for he has witnessed them." ...

But when David's place was empty again the next day, Saul asked Jonathan, "Why hasn't the son of Jesse been here for the meal either yesterday or today?"

Jonathan replied, "David earnestly asked me if he could go to Bethlehem. He said, 'Please let me go, for we are having a family sacrifice. My brother demanded that I be there. So please let me get away to see my brothers.' That's why he isn't here at the king's table."

Saul boiled with rage at Jonathan. "You stupid son of a whore!" he swore at him. "Do you think I don't know that you want him to be king in your place, shaming yourself and your mother? As long as that son of Jesse is alive, you'll never be king. Now go and get him so I can kill him!" ...

The next morning, as agreed, Jonathan went out into the field and took a young boy with him to gather his arrows. "Start running," he told the boy, "so you can find the arrows as I shoot them." So the boy ran, and Jonathan shot an arrow beyond him. When the boy had almost reached the arrow, Jonathan shouted, "The arrow is still ahead of you. Hurry, hurry, don't wait." So the boy quickly gathered up the arrows and ran back to his master. He, of course, suspected nothing; only Jonathan and David understood the signal. Then Jonathan gave his bow and arrows to the boy and told him to take them back to town.

As soon as the boy was gone, David came out from where he had been hiding near the stone pile. Then David bowed three times to Jonathan with his face to the ground. Both of them were in tears as they embraced each other and said good-bye, especially David.

At last Jonathan said to David, "Go in peace, for we have sworn loyalty to each other in the LORD's name. The LORD is the witness of a bond between us and our children forever." Then David left, and Jonathan returned to the town. (1 Sam. 20:16–23, 27–31, 35–42)

Looking at the highlighted areas, what stands out to you most? Why?

Even in reading this, you can feel the weight of this moment. Jonathan was telling his best friend to run for his life. They suspected (and they ended up being right) that this was probably a "goodbye forever" moment as David plunged into the wilderness and Jonathan headed back to the palace. It's hard to imagine how heartbreaking this all must have been for David. He had been abandoned by everyone.

Maybe you can sympathize. Perhaps you, too, have felt the sting of betrayal. People you've loved have walked out on you. Places of assumed safety came with hurt and risk. A friend has become your enemy, a family member is still holding on to a grudge, and you have had to walk away from a relationship that meant the world to you. We have all been hurt. We have all hurt others. *The unfortunate truth we all learn is that people—ourselves included—aren't perfect. The good news, however, is that God is. Although people hurt and abandon us, He never will.*

What adjectives would you use to describe the way David felt?

If you have been betrayed or abandoned, how would you describe your own experience?

Open your Bible to Romans 8:38–39, and fill in the blanks:

> And I am convinced that _____ can ever separate us from God's love. Neither _____ nor _____, neither _____ nor _____, neither _____ for today nor _____ about tomorrow—not even the _____ can separate us from God's love. No _____ in the sky above or in the earth below—indeed, _____ in all creation will ever be able to separate us from the love of God that is revealed in Christ Jesus our Lord.

Take a moment to add your own twist to this verse. What is causing you to feel separated from the love of God? Write it in the blank, and then read the statement aloud.

I'm convinced that not even _____ can ever separate me from God's love.

When we start to lose heart, we can run into the wide-open arms of God. There, we will always find safety and a place to belong.

CLOSE-UP

Spoiler alert: David was about to enter some of the loneliest years of his life. But he knew he was not alone. God was with him.

I bet that while David was on the run, he would often think of his best friend, Jonathan, a truer brother than his own biological brothers. They should have been laughing together around a fire, sharing a meal, or practicing with their weapons in a friendly duel, but instead they were separated by a king's madness. Yet they couldn't change their circumstances.

While they were driven apart because of Saul, Jonathan and David always seemed to be tied together in spirit. Jonathan was always on David's team, no matter what. I'm sure you know someone like that.

Who has been a "Jonathan" in your life? How does it feel to have someone in your corner who has remained with you when others have left?

Who are *you* being a Jonathan for?

Even while David's cheeks were wet with tears as he left Jonathan and went into hiding, he could sense that God's eyes were on him and that God's presence was with him. God was tangibly by David's side, and that is certainly what got him through even the loneliest of nights.

What does it mean to you personally that God will never leave you and that nothing can ever separate you from His love?

CHANGE DIRECTION

When we allow hardship to take our eyes off God, we begin heading in the wrong direction, chasing solace and comfort. When we find ourselves in a bad place, it's important to remember that we're not stuck. We can change direction. That's exactly what David did.

Running for his life, David headed toward a place called Gath. Gath was where the Philistines, the enemies of Israel (remember Goliath?), hung out. Of course, when David came strolling through the enemy camp, they recognized him.

Read 1 Samuel 21:10–12, and answer the following:

What did the servants of Achish say to David?

DIRECTOR'S CUT: HE CARES FOR US

I'm not writing this Bible study while living in a vacuum or an ivory tower. I face the same pain that everyone faces. More than sixteen years ago, my oldest son, Christopher, was in a tragic automobile accident and departed to Heaven. To have my son suddenly taken from us was devastating. I didn't feel like I could even survive it. I thought hearing those words would literally cause me to die, but God was there for me. When I called out to the Lord, He sustained me in my hour of pain, just as He did with David, and He sustains me to this very day.

When 1 Peter 5:7 says, "Give all your worries and cares to God, for he cares about you," the idea is that we deliberately cease to worry and

How did David feel?

Props

©Eleonora Tuveri/iStock/Getty Images Plus

Did David really think he would blend in with the Philistines? At this point, David was a legend. The Philistines had seen him on the battlefield and knew he'd won great victories against them. As a warrior, he was the GOAT (greatest of all time). He was famous. There were songs about him. His merchandise was everywhere. So what was David even thinking? Possibly, he was so preoccupied with his problems that he wasn't thinking, or maybe he believed that somehow no one would know who he was. At least he knew Saul's men would not be too quick to chase him there.

FORESHADOWING

Another great man in the Bible—one of Jesus' disciples, Simon Peter—did this same thing. After Jesus was arrested, Peter was standing by the bonfire in the dark thinking he would not be identified as one of Jesus' followers. But there in the fire's glow, a woman said,

> "This man was one of Jesus' followers!"
> But Peter denied it. "Woman," he said, "I don't even know him!"
> After a while someone else looked at him and said, "You must be one of them!"
> "No, man, I'm not!" Peter retorted.

put everything into the hands of the Lord.

There will be a time when you, too, will lose a loved one. You'll say, "I know they're in Heaven. I know I'll see them again. I know they're in perfect joy and happiness." For a while, you'll be okay. But then *boom*, another thought will come and you'll go down again, because that is how grief works. It rolls over us like waves.

When hardship hits and overtakes you and you need to get your head back to the surface for a gulp of air and perspective, cast your cares upon God. Roll with what you're facing, and let God assume the responsibility for your welfare. He won't let your circumstances take you under or cause you to drown.

About an hour later someone else insisted, "This must be one of them, because he is a Galilean, too."

But Peter said, "Man, I don't know what you are talking about." (Luke 22:56–60)

How are Peter's and David's actions similar? Why do you think they thought they could hide in plain sight?

What is it about us humans that when hardship or tragedy strikes, we drift toward unhealthy spaces rather than keeping our eyes on God? Why don't we allow Him to lead us to the safety and hope we long for? When our life is shattered, we isolate instead of seeking community within our church. We feel spiritually dead, so we call up an acquaintance who feels the same way to hang out with rather than calling our wise friend who will point us toward Jesus. To numb our sorrows, we may turn to alcohol or jump into a binge-watching hole rather than bringing our struggles to the light.

At some point, David realized his idea to go to Gath had gone horribly wrong. So he devised a "crazy" escape plan. Read about it in 1 Samuel 21:13–15.

What did David pretend to be?

What did he do?

What did Achish believe?

"Madman" was not a good look for David, but he escaped and fled to the cave of Adullam. In this hiding place, David wrote Psalm 142:

> I cry out to the LORD;
>> I plead for the LORD's mercy.
> I pour out my complaints before him
>> and tell him all my troubles.
> When I am overwhelmed,
>> you alone know the way I should turn.
> Wherever I go,
>> my enemies have set traps for me.
> I look for someone to come and help me,
>> but no one gives me a passing thought!
> No one will help me;
>> no one cares a bit what happens to me.
> Then I pray to you, O LORD;
>> I say, "You are my place of refuge.
>> You are all I really want in life."
> Hear my cry,
>> for I am very low.
> Rescue me from my persecutors,
>> for they are too strong for me.
> Bring me out of prison
>> so I can thank you.
> The godly will crowd around me,
>> for you are good to me.

Looking at the highlighted areas, what stands out to you most? Why?

BREAKING THE FOURTH WALL

In hindsight everything is twenty-twenty, right? I definitely shouldn't have gone into Philistine territory. I thought it might be clever to hide in plain sight, but clearly I was wrong. I had to pretend to be someone that I wasn't just to break free. It was humiliating.

Have you ever headed in the wrong direction for solace or comfort? What did you find that person or place actually offered you?

I put myself in the wrong place at the wrong time. God didn't tell me to go there; I just went. I should have sought His advice. If I had taken His path, maybe I wouldn't have had to encounter Achish and the Philistines. Take time to learn from my actions by answering these questions:

What does it look like for you to be totally honest with God about how you feel right now?

How can you seek Jesus and move in the right direction when life seems to be going wrong?

Have you ever felt the way David did as he was writing this psalm? Do you feel that way right now?

Notice how David shifted gears in the middle of the psalm. He went from his one-person pity party to noticing what God was doing in the midst of his struggle. He ended with the hopeful statement, "The godly will crowd around me, for you are good to me."

So, what should we do when things fall apart? We must focus on God, not our problems. We learn from David that it's okay to say to the Lord, "I don't really like this situation I'm in. I don't like the circumstances that surround me. I don't want this. Lord, help me."

While we can be totally honest with God about how we feel, we must also remind our souls that this is part of God's plan and purpose for our lives. We have to hold on to hope more than our hardship.

Let's come back to Johnny Cash. Earlier, we talked about his brother, Jack. Amazingly, Jack Cash survived the accident in the sawmill, but everyone knew, because of the extent of his injuries, that he was not long for this world. As Jack was in the hospital room, surrounded by his family, he was given a glimpse of glory.

Jack said to his mother, "Mama, do you hear the angels?" He then turned to his hard, faithless father and asked, "Ray, will you meet me in Heaven?" At that moment, Ray Cash fell to his knees and asked God to forgive him of his sins, and he put his faith in Jesus Christ. Jack died of his wounds a week later at just fifteen years old.[3]

Johnny went on to have a very successful music career, as we know. What not many people know was that it was largely shaped by the loss of his brother, which transformed him into "the man in black."

He had his ups and downs. In his later years, Johnny made a deeper commitment to follow Jesus Christ as his career and health seemed to be taking a downturn. In this valley, a producer named Rick Rubin felt that Johnny wasn't getting his due. He wanted to lift Johnny back up and believed his music should still be in the spotlight. With Rubin, Johnny made *American Recordings*, a series of records that were released starting in 1994 (which, in my opinion, are some of the best recordings of his career), culminating with a song called "Hurt" that became an award-winning hit in 2002.

"Hurt" was Johnny's swan song, his final public declaration that while his life had been hard, he always longed to keep true to his heart. He could see how every earthly thing passes away and that the most prized possession we have is life itself.

As a producer, I had the honor of working on a project about Johnny's life. I also wrote a book about his spiritual journey. The documentary film we made featured country artists like Tim McGraw, Wynonna Judd, Sheryl Crow, and others talking about the impact of Johnny's life on them. Marty Stuart, a close friend of Johnny's, narrated the film. It seemed Johnny wanted to leave us all with a final thought—a question, really. Johnny's sister, Joanne, shared this story in the film *Johnny Cash: The Redemption of an American Icon.*

> One day toward the end of his life, Johnny called me over to his home and asked me, "If you walked on the shores of Galilee and you looked up and saw Jesus walking toward you, what do you think He'd say to you?" Chills went all over me. I didn't know how to answer it. Johnny looked me in the eye and said, "He would say to you, 'Feed My sheep.'"[4]

Johnny Cash knew what David knew: *You can do everything wrong; you can gain the world or lose it all. But the full life God offers is the greatest gift.* If we've been going in the wrong direction, we can always reroute and begin to run straight toward Jesus.

David's Diary

Slowly and reflectively read the following psalm aloud.

Psalm 34

I will praise the LORD at all times.
    I will constantly speak his praises.
I will boast only in the LORD;
    let all who are helpless take heart.
Come, let us tell of the LORD's greatness;
    let us exalt his name together.

I prayed to the LORD, and he answered me.
    He freed me from all my fears.
Those who look to him for help will be radiant with joy;
    no shadow of shame will darken their faces.

In my desperation I prayed, and the LORD listened;
    he saved me from all my troubles.
For the angel of the LORD is a guard;
    he surrounds and defends all who fear him.

Taste and see that the LORD is good;
    Oh, the joys of those who take refuge in him!
Fear the LORD, you his godly people,
    for those who fear him will have all they need.
Even strong young lions sometimes go hungry,
    but those who trust in the LORD will lack no good thing.

Come, my children, and listen to me,
    and I will teach you to fear the LORD.
Does anyone want to live a life
    that is long and prosperous?
Then keep your tongue from speaking evil
    and your lips from telling lies!
Turn away from evil and do good.
    Search for peace, and work to maintain it.

The eyes of the LORD watch over those who do right;
    his ears are open to their cries for help.
But the LORD turns his face against those who do evil;
    he will erase their memory from the earth.
The LORD hears his people when they call to him for help.
    He rescues them from all their troubles.
The LORD is close to the brokenhearted;
    he rescues those whose spirits are crushed.

The righteous person faces many troubles,
    but the LORD comes to the rescue each time.
For the LORD protects the bones of the righteous;
    not one of them is broken!

Calamity will surely destroy the wicked,
and those who hate the righteous will be punished.
But the LORD will redeem those who serve him.
No one who takes refuge in him will be condemned.

Think deeply about what you just read. Use all your senses, emotions, and imagination to interact with this psalm. Feel free to underline words or doodle or write.

Respond to all you've received. Take a moment to compile your thoughts and turn them into a prayer to God. Begin with this prayer, and use the rest of the space to run with your own. You can pray out loud, with others, or silently in your heart.

Jesus, there are times when I'm more cowardly than coura-geous and I bow down in fear instead of standing up boldly in faith. Help me recall all the giants You've helped me slay and remember that I can put my faith and trust in You.

I also know You will never leave me or forsake me. Thank You for standing by me at all times, even in moments where I've pushed away from You. When I look in the wrong direction for comfort during life's problems, You remind me that You are my true safe haven. When life seems to be going wrong, You can make it right.

Thank You for making me brave and keeping me safe, even in the middle of life's greatest battles.

In Jesus' name I pray, amen.

Personal Psalm Writing

Following David's "I'm-struggling-and-yet-I-trust" pattern, write your own psalm here. If you're having a hard time getting started, see the end of lesson 1 for ideas of how you might organize your psalm.

WHAT KING WILL YOU FOLLOW?

I am still king. Remember this.
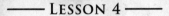

KING SAUL, SEASON 1, EPISODE 2, HOUSE OF DAVID

> *And so, dear brothers and sisters, I plead with*
> *you to give your bodies to God because of all he*
> *has done for you. Let them be a living and holy*
> *sacrifice—the kind he will find acceptable. This*
> *is truly the way to worship him. Don't copy the*
> *behavior and customs of this world, but let God*
> *transform you into a new person by changing the*
> *way you think. Then you will learn to know God's*
> *will for you, which is good and pleasing and perfect.*
>
> ROMANS 12:1–2

THE WAY THE DEVIL DEALS

Once upon a time, there was a hunter out in the forest who discovered exactly what he was looking for: a giant bear. He pulled out his loaded rifle, got into a shooting stance, and put the bear in his sights. Just as he exhaled and began to squeeze the trigger, the bear began to speak: "Excuse me. Isn't it better to talk than to shoot?"

The hunter was shocked and speechless. The bear continued, "Can we negotiate the matter? Tell me, what is it you're looking for?"

"Well, a fur coat," the hunter replied honestly.

"Ah," said the bear. "Now we're getting somewhere, because what I want is a full stomach. Let's negotiate." So they disappeared into the forest together.

Apparently, the negotiations were successful, because after a little time passed, the bear came out from the forest alone. It turned out that they both got what they wanted. The bear got his full stomach, and the hunter got a fur coat.

This is how deals with the Devil work. Listen, Satan is wicked, evil, and cunning. He's been honing his craft for a long time, so he's really good at what he does. He knows he can't generally bring down a believer in Jesus with one strike. Therefore, he seeks to dismantle believers a little at a time through the subtle strategy of compromise. He's been using this tactic since Adam and Eve were in the garden (Gen. 3), and he'll be using it until he's cast into the lake of fire at the end of time (Rev. 20:10). So we cannot be surprised when we see the Devil try to use it to bring David down.

Throughout his life, David faced temptation time and time again. For example, Satan incited him to disobey God (1 Chron. 21:1). Then, centuries later, Satan used something of David's to try to tempt Jesus Himself: Satan misinterpreted Psalm 91 (which scholars think was written by Moses but compiled by David) to tempt Jesus in the desert (Matt. 4:6).

We left off in our last lesson with David in the cave of Adullam. He had to flee from Saul's jealous rage, leave his wife and best friend behind, pretend to be crazy, and finally hide in the cave. There he had time alone. No one was with him. But David would emerge from this cave a different person.

I'm sure he was feeling sorry for himself, thinking, *Man, I just did what God called me to do. I was happy watching my little flock of sheep. How did this come on me? This isn't fair. This isn't right.* But notice how, just as he was getting down and lonely, God surrounded him.

Read 1 Samuel 22:1–2, and answer these questions:

Where did David escape to?

Who went to meet him there?

How many men were with him?

Remember, David's father, Jesse, wouldn't acknowledge the existence of his son when the prophet Samuel came to Bethlehem looking for the next king of Israel. In a stunning twist of events, now David's whole family has come to join him. That must have been strange but reassuring to David.

Satan is the king of isolation. He wants us to remain alone because then he can be the main voice in our ear. On the other hand, God is the God of community and reconciliation. Sometimes we, like David, drift apart from people. We might not see members of our family or close friends from our younger days for years. We may not even know why we're not talking to them anymore. But then something happens that brings us together. We start communicating again, and fellowship is restored.

Have you ever experienced reconciliation with a friend or family member? What happened? What did it feel like to reconnect?

Props

This is similar to what happened with David.

Can you imagine their reunion conversation? "David, we really under-estimated you as a kid. You're not just the weird brother watching the sheep, writing songs. You're a warrior. You're going to be the next king! I know we weren't always behind you, but we are now."

©Mint Images RF/Getty Images

We know David was a man of integrity because he handled success very well. *One of the greatest tests of a person's character is not failure but success.*

When some people receive power, money, or authority, it goes to their head. They become an altogether different person. David was still hiding in a cave, it's true. But he wasn't alone anymore, and he was becoming a war chief with a growing army of supporters. Yet he was still that humble, loving, caring young man who was described as "a man after God's own heart."

Take a look back at 1 Samuel 22:2. It wasn't just his family who showed up. Everyone who was in distress, in debt, or discontented gathered to him. And he became captain over about four hundred men. Wow! What a motley crew. This was a ragtag army.

God seems to specialize in turning outcasts into men and women of God.

We often put the people we read about in the Bible on pedestals. However, they weren't special. They were just like you and me. Let's look at Jesus' twelve disciples as an example.

We look at the apostles and think, *They were so amazing.* However, you can read any of the Gospels (Matthew, Mark, Luke, or John) and discover that Peter was a hotheaded, impulsive, and an outspoken guy. James and John were not called "the Sons of Thunder" for nothing (Mark 3:17): on one occasion, they wanted to call fire down from Heaven on a city that was not hospitable toward them (Luke 9:54). Then there's Matthew, the tax collector (Matt. 9:9): he was working for the occupying force of Rome and considered a traitor by his fellow Jews. And Simon, as a zealot, was dedicated to the violent overthrow of Rome (Luke 6:15).

So Jesus took His own motley crew of misfits and transformed them into the apostles, and they turned the world upside down with the radical love of God. Check out how the apostle Paul summed it up in 1 Corinthians 1:26, and fill in the blanks:

> Remember, dear brothers and sisters, that few of you were _____ in
> the world's eyes or _____ or _____ when God called you.

Isn't it obvious that God deliberately chooses men and women that the culture overlooks, exploits, and abuses? *God chooses the outcasts to expose the hollow pretensions of the proud.*

As David looked around at his mighty men, he began to again gain perspective, and he sat down and wrote Psalm 57:

> Have mercy on me, O God, have mercy!
>   I look to you for protection.
> I will hide beneath the shadow of your wings
>   until the danger passes by.
> I cry out to God Most High,
>   to God who will fulfill his purpose for me.

He will send help from heaven to rescue me,
   disgracing those who hound me.
My God will send forth his unfailing love and faithfulness.

I am surrounded by fierce lions
   who greedily devour human prey—
whose teeth pierce like spears and arrows,
   and whose tongues cut like swords.

Be exalted, O God, above the highest heavens!
   May your glory shine over all the earth.

My enemies have set a trap for me.
   I am weary from distress.
They have dug a deep pit in my path,
   but they themselves have fallen into it.

My heart is confident in you, O God;
   my heart is confident.
   No wonder I can sing your praises!
Wake up, my heart!
   Wake up, O lyre and harp!
   I will wake the dawn with my song.
I will thank you, Lord, among all the people.
   I will sing your praises among the nations.
For your unfailing love is as high as the heavens.
   Your faithfulness reaches to the clouds.

Be exalted, O God, above the highest heavens.
   May your glory shine over all the earth.

Of the highlighted portions of this psalm, what stands out to you the most? Why?

Instead of focusing on the failure he and his outcast army were seemingly facing, David chose to believe for the victory to come. This is just like when God looked upon David's brothers and told Samuel, "The LORD doesn't see things the way you see them. People judge by outward appearance, but the LORD looks at the heart" (1 Sam. 16:7). David was looking at the heart of his people and standing on hope. Thank God, this is what the Lord does for us all.

Let it sink in that God sees you differently from how you see yourself. We see a blank canvas; God sees a finished painting. We see a failure; God sees potential. We see the past; God sees the future. We see a mess; God sees a message. We see a zero; God sees a potential hero.

Take a moment to look up the following Bible verses and match them to the way God sees you.

Jeremiah 31:3   I have been made complete
through Jesus Christ.

John 15:5   I am wonderfully made.

Colossians 2:10   I am helped by God.

Ephesians 1:5   I am rescued.

Hebrews 4:16   I am a child of God.

Colossians 3:12   I am tenderly loved.

Colossians 1:13   I am chosen.

Psalm 139:14   I am a friend of God.

Circle the verses or phrases that stand out to you the most.

Satan always tempts us to look through his own warped lens rather than through God's perfect perspective. This is the way Satan deals. But remember: *We always have a choice about whose lens we look through.*

This, too, was one of David's great tests. When we look at Psalm 57, we see that he stated, "My heart is confident in you" (v. 7). David passed the test and, through all his mistakes and mishaps, remained focused on God. He set his sights on his heavenly purpose and moved toward the throne of Israel.

GOD'S WILL, GOD'S WAY, IN GOD'S TIME

There's a saying that goes, "You're always sailing into or out of a storm." I think it's true. Just because David decided to follow God wholeheartedly didn't mean Satan would stop dealing him temptations or throwing obstacles in his path.

Still on the run for his life, David left his family with the king of Moab while he waited to hear from God. He encountered a prophet named Gad who told him to go to Judah. So David began to head that way by going into the forest of Hereth.

Meanwhile, Saul, who was still on the warpath for David, seemed to dive into manic episodes. He ordered eighty-five priests to be killed because he falsely believed that David was after him and that the priests were keeping him hidden. He gathered his army and did everything in his power to catch David. But then he took a break from tracking down David and ducked into a cave.

BREAKING THE FOURTH WALL

Not that I ever really had you fooled, but I know you're starting to see that I was just an imperfect guy who carried the anointing of God. I was an outcast from day one, and while I was on the run, God surrounded me with more people who were distressed and put out. Together, we made quite the rabble, but at least I wasn't alone anymore. God surrounded me.

As a leader, I realized that I set the culture for this group. Were we going to be down-and-out, complaining about the hand that had been dealt to us? Or were we going to adopt God's view of us and realize that we were chosen to stand together as family and friends to fight for freedom? Thank God, we decided to look to Him for our identity because, from here, many more challenges presented themselves.

If we hadn't had God's perspective, we probably wouldn't have made the right choices. I certainly wouldn't have. What about you? How has agreeing (or not) with God's view of your situation affected the choices you've made?

In what ways have you felt drawn to adopt Satan's view of yourself, others, your problems, or your blessings? Why is it tempting to adopt his view over God's perspective?

Do you see yourself as part of the outcasts in my story? Or do you view yourself as more of a qualified army member? Why is this so?

BREAKING THE FOURTH WALL

Truthfully, it would have been awesome if God would have given me the go-ahead to kill Saul right then and there in that cave. I wouldn't have had to be on the run anymore. My days as an outlaw would have come to an end. In that moment, I could have transferred from outcast to king.

However, I knew that if I took matters into my own hands, I would be no different from Saul. I learned exactly what not to do by watching him lead. If you want to follow God, you definitely do not seek your own will and glory. I've seen firsthand that God won't bless any personal power trips. So I had to trust His timing over my own.

In my heart, I felt so convicted about following God that I even second-guessed some of my decisions. Should I have cut Saul's robe to prove a point? I'm still not sure about that one. But the important thing is that I didn't seek my own will. I left it in the hands of God, and, as you'll see later in my story, that did work out for His glory and my good.

But I'm wondering … if you were me and encountered Saul in the cave, what would you have done? Why is that?

I never got to ask Saul what he learned from all his actions. But I think he would have told us that he and Satan both fell due to their longing to establish their own glory and take matters into their own hands.

How does this serve as a warning for us?

Let's take a moment and learn from my decision in the cave with Saul and surrender what God needs to control. What are you struggling to place in God's hands? What does it look like for you to trust God to do His will His way in His time?

Read 1 Samuel 24:1–7, and recount what took place.

How many men did Saul take to look for David?

Where were David and his men when Saul went into the cave?

What did the men tell David to do?

What did David do instead?

How did David reply to his men?

How would you have instructed David in this moment?

Isn't that an interesting twist in the story? This was David's moment! Saul had been pursuing David for years, trying to take his life by throwing javelins at him and pursuing him with armies. And here Saul had fallen right into David's hands. He could have finally ended it and taken his rightful place on the throne. David had to choose: Was he going to do this his way or God's way?

FORESHADOWING

David's submission to God's will reflects the same heart Jesus had in the garden of Gethsemane just before He was arrested and crucified. He was always praying that, despite our human tendency to want to take matters into our own hands, God's will would be done. Take a look at the following verses, and write down how you see David's posture reflected in Jesus' thoughts and actions.

Matthew 26:36–46

Saul reminds us of the Devil, who pursues us constantly. He doesn't let up either. Wouldn't it be nice if Satan took a day off? "Hey, Devil, could you take Mondays off? Just don't bother me." Unfortunately, he doesn't even seem to go on a lunch break. He's always seeking his prey.

What does the Bible warn us to do in 1 Peter 5:8? In this verse, what is the Devil doing?

In the book of Job, there's a striking scene in which the angels of God appear before the Lord— and Satan is among them. Now we think, what's the Devil doing in Heaven?

The Devil is not what culture makes him out to be. He doesn't have red skin, horns, a goatee (why do they always give him a goatee?), and a pointed tail. He's not some caricature that a cartoonist came up with. The reality is the Devil is (or at least began as) a beautiful angel. Lucifer (which translates to "the shining one") is how he was recognized in Heaven, but he rebelled against the Lord.

Read the following key verses, and make notes about what they reveal about the origins and character of our adversary, the Devil:

Luke 10:18

Revelation 12:7–9

Isaiah 14:12–15

Ezekiel 28:11–19

You might be surprised to know that the Devil believes the Bible is true. Now, he hates it. He's opposed to everything it says. But he has no doubts about it. He especially knows what the Bible says about his own ultimate judgment when he will face the wrath of God: he will be thrown into the lake of fire (Rev. 12).

Why is Satan so angry? Why is he agitated? Why is he pursuing us? Because he knows his days are numbered. King Saul had this same realization. He knew his days as king were numbered, and he couldn't let it go. David could also have aligned with Satan in that moment in the cave and said, "Hey, you know, I'm just tired of this. I'll give God a little assistance and take my own glory."

But David chose to align with God's timing and to prioritize God's will above his own. He trusted that God would accomplish His will in His way and on His own schedule.

Ecclesiastes 3:11 reminds us that "God has made everything beautiful for its own time." But truly trusting that, like David chose to do, is hard. We get impatient with God, don't we?

When our spouse hasn't come to know the Lord, we make plans to nag them into Heaven, which inevitably keeps them even further away from the church.

When our prodigal child hasn't returned, we push them away by overly pursuing them.

When we haven't received what we've been praying for, we throw in the towel on waiting and settle for something outside of God's will for us, leaving us even more disappointed and dissatisfied.

Do any of these scenarios sound familiar to you? What have you grown impatient with God about?

Here's what was happening with David: Saul was still technically king. David decided to do God's will, God's way, in God's time, and he didn't kill Saul when he had the chance. He knew that God had put Saul on the throne and that it wasn't his job to take Saul out. His conscience began bothering him after he'd only cut Saul's robe. This is evidence of David's tender heart.

The state of David's heart was what made him different from Saul. The only thing that really separated his life decisions from Saul's was that he was willing to allow God to accomplish what God desired in his life. *While Saul took matters into his own hands, David placed his life in the hands of God.*

When faced with the choice between our own will and God's, what will we choose?

VENGEANCE IS NEVER OURS

David choosing to not take vengeance against Saul might be hard for us to comprehend because we live in a culture that believes in the adage "Don't get mad; get even." In our world of conflict, division and discord are everywhere. This is amplified on social media. It seems as if payback is always the answer, never forgiveness. However, God commands us to forgive.

Read the following verses, and write down what God instructs us to do:

Romans 12:14

Ephesians 4:32

Romans 12:18

Instead of taking vengeance, we are called to extend forgiveness. Scripture doesn't just suggest this; it commands it.

I don't know about you, but forgiveness doesn't come naturally to me. I'll be the first to confess: If you hit me, I want to hit you. If you insult me, I want to have a better insult to throw back. However, God tells me to forgive. In the Lord's Prayer, Jesus gave us this example when He prayed, "Forgive us our sins, as we have forgiven those who sin against us" (Matt. 6:12). What Jesus is really saying here is this: *forgiven people should be forgiving people.*

On this topic, C. S. Lewis also bluntly stated, "Everyone says forgiveness is a lovely idea, until they have something to forgive."[1] We want to be forgiven ourselves, but when someone hurts us, we want them to get what they deserve. Holding a grudge or trying to judge someone for the wrongs committed against you binds you to the person or action. Forgiveness, on the other hand, actually offers you freedom.

Time magazine did a cover story titled "Should All Be Forgiven?" Its team scientifically proved that forgiveness is good for us not only spiritually but also physically. They discovered that forgiving people mends marriages, removes depression, and makes life easier in every area.[2] Looks like science is catching up to the Bible.

Though David didn't have access to the science, the quotes, and the biblical references available to us, he innately knew he had to extend forgiveness to Saul. He demonstrated the power of this grace when, after Saul had done his business in the cave, he yelled something similar to "Hey, King Saul, do you notice a little draft? I'm holding a piece of your robe right here. I was so close I could have killed you. But I didn't!" Saul's entire countenance changed as a result.

Read 1 Samuel 24:16–22, and record what happened by answering the following:

What did Saul do when he heard David's voice?

What did Saul confess to David?

What did Saul ask David to swear?

How did David react?

Where did David and Saul go when they parted ways?

This is a huge improvement over the murderous language Saul had been throwing around. Unfortunately, his kindness was short-lived. He said these things but apparently didn't really mean them because, shortly after this, he returned to his angry, manic ways.

People say, "The proof is in the pudding." I don't know what that means, because I've eaten pudding and I've never found proof in it. But I think the idea is, if someone really is sorry, they'll change. If they don't actually change, are they sorry? The answer is no.

What does 2 Corinthians 7:10 say about godly sorrow?

We can know that King Saul's tears were not from repentance because he continued down his path of sin and destruction.

Pay attention to the end of this chapter, 1 Samuel 24. David was not a fool. He didn't just take Saul at his word and go home with him. He kept his distance. Why? Because he'd had a few javelins thrown in his direction. He didn't trust Saul, and he was right not to. Saul went back to the palace with no intention of abdicating his throne. David retreated to the stronghold, a place of refuge, safety, and concealment.

The Devil wants us to take vengeance into our own hands, while God asks us to release it. He is our hiding place until the storm blows over.

What did David call the Lord in Psalm 27:1?

David keenly knew God to be his safe place, and we need to know the same. While the Devil wants us to build our own thrones, God wants us to trust that He is on the throne and is working all things out, redeeming our stories, and bringing about the justice we seek for our hurt and pain.

CLOSE-UP

Whether it was because his brothers bullied him when he was a kid or because he was treated like a servant while working bottom-of-the-ladder jobs, David always seemed to know that not forgiving people only hurts you in the end. The weight of a grudge is heavy, and it will drag you down. When you forgive and allow God to bring about justice, you are set free. But that initial release is tough. Our human nature seeks vengeance, while our spirit knows that only God can truly set things right.

Why do you think it's so hard to forgive people?

Whom do you personally need to forgive so that you can be free?

What does it look like for you to trust God to bring about the justice you seek for your hurt and pain?

WHICH KING WILL YOU FOLLOW?

I have five grandchildren: one grandson and four grand-daughters. Boys are very different from girls—and have vastly different requests for Christmas and birthday gifts. When I asked my grandson, "What would you like for Christmas?" he replied, "A snake." Nothing proclaims the birth of Jesus like a serpent, right? So I bought him a black king snake that lives in a secure cage that the family put ten feet away from their hamster's cage. He named him Inky.

The other day, my grandson's father said to him, "Hey, buddy. Uh, have you checked on your hamster lately? Does he have enough water and food?" So Christopher went and checked the hamster's cage but couldn't find him anywhere. What he did find was the snake. Somehow the king snake had gotten out of his cage and slithered into the hamster's cage.

BREAKING THE FOURTH WALL

I lived in an era when all the lands had kings. Some kings were good, and others, like Saul, carried a bad reputation. Many were tyrants who let power go to their heads. They demanded absolute submission and forced their people to worship them.

Here's what I can tell you for sure—our God is a great king. He's always true to His word, is at work for the good of His people, and loves us deeply. He guides us like a humble shepherd yet defends us like the mightiest warrior. Though He offers us so much, you must still decide:

Which king will you follow?

Is there any area where you realize you have made a deal with the Devil, agreeing with his "truth" over God's Word? Describe it.

Is there any area where you've allowed the Devil to gain a foothold through a repetitive sin or unforgiveness? What do you think God is asking you to do about it?

I imagine a conversation took place. The snake said to the hamster, "Tell me what you're looking for." The hamster said, "Well, I would like to have a snakeskin coat." "Excellent," said the snake. "I would like a full stomach." Apparently, the negotiations were successful. The hamster got his snakeskin coat, and the snake got a full stomach.

We're coming back to that story because we have a tendency to forget that the Devil is cunning. He's a master manipulator who is really good at getting into the little openings in our lives. If you give him an inch, he'll take a mile. Then he gets a foothold in your life.

I wrote a book called *Lennon, Dylan, Alice, & Jesus*, about the spiritual journeys of different rock stars. Some people who hadn't read the book literally judged the book by its cover, saying, "Greg, don't you know these people have sold their souls to the Devil?" I don't even know where the idea came from that the Devil appears with a shiny contract and says, "Hey, I'll make you a famous rock star and give you all the success in the world if you sign this." Then, they "sign their soul away."

We can't actually sign our souls away, because they don't belong to us; they belong to God. However, you can (in a sense) make a deal with the Devil. You can live the way he wants you to live, effectively putting yourself under his control. Unfortunately, you don't get anything good out of the bargain!

Here's the good news: When Jesus died on the cross and shed His blood for your sins, He broke the control of the Devil in your life. From the moment you choose to accept Jesus' free gift of salvation, all satanic deals are off. Isn't that great?

Take a look at Colossians 2:13–14, and fill in the blanks.

> You were _____ because of your sins and because your sinful nature
> was not yet cut away. Then God made you _____ with
> Christ, for he _____ all our sins. He
> _____ the record of the charges against us and
> _____ by nailing it to the cross.

We no longer live in bondage to sin because He canceled the record of charges against us by nailing it to the cross. Satan can't bind us to any agreement with sin if we choose to agree with Jesus.

Just as we have to decide to follow Jesus, so the people of Israel had a choice in David's time. Which king did they want to follow? Wicked King Saul or godly King David? We have the same choice in our life: Which king are we going to follow? Are we going to follow Jesus Christ, the King of Kings and Lord of Lords? Or are we going to follow Satan?

You may think you have other options. *What if I just follow my own course? I can be the captain of my ship.* No, you can't. Your ship is sinking, Captain. You're taking on water. The Bible describes the Devil as the god of this world who is in control of the lives of those who do not yet believe (see 2 Cor. 4:4). He captains our lives when our faith in God has holes in it.

It's Christ who sets us free because of the blood He shed on the cross and the life He offers us through His resurrection. If we decide to follow this King, He will take us into His kingdom.

Remember the criminal on the cross next to Jesus? What did he say to Jesus in Luke 23:42?

How did Jesus respond in verse 43?

At the last moment, that man believed and was forgiven of all his sin. This can happen for us too. We must take inventory of our lives to see if we have given the Devil a foothold in any area.

Circle any statement below that is true of your life:

I have a sin that is a part of my life on a regular basis.

I want revenge.

I am holding a grudge.

I am angry and bitter because someone I loved hurt me.

Someone has taken something unfairly from me, and I want to even the score.

Take time to acknowledge this and to forgive the people involved. *Don't let what happened to you have power over you. Forgive and put it behind you so that you, like David, can move on and pursue your God-given calling.*

David's Diary

Slowly and reflectively read the following psalm aloud.

Psalm 40

I waited patiently for the LORD to help me,
and he turned to me and heard my cry.
He lifted me out of the pit of despair,
out of the mud and the mire.
He set my feet on solid ground
and steadied me as I walked along.
He has given me a new song to sing,
a hymn of praise to our God.
Many will see what he has done and be amazed.
They will put their trust in the LORD.

Oh, the joys of those who trust the LORD,
who have no confidence in the proud
or in those who worship idols.
O LORD my God, you have performed many wonders for us.
Your plans for us are too numerous to list.
You have no equal.
If I tried to recite all your wonderful deeds,
I would never come to the end of them.

You take no delight in sacrifices or offerings.
Now that you have made me listen, I finally understand—
you don't require burnt offerings or sin offerings.
Then I said, "Look, I have come.
As is written about me in the Scriptures:
I take joy in doing your will, my God,
for your instructions are written on my heart."

I have told all your people about your justice.
  I have not been afraid to speak out,
    as you, O LORD, well know.
I have not kept the good news of your justice hidden in my heart;
  I have talked about your faithfulness and saving power.
I have told everyone in the great assembly
  of your unfailing love and faithfulness.

LORD, don't hold back your tender mercies from me.
  Let your unfailing love and faithfulness always protect me.
For troubles surround me—
  too many to count!
My sins pile up so high
  I can't see my way out.
They outnumber the hairs on my head.
  I have lost all courage.

Please, LORD, rescue me!
  Come quickly, LORD, and help me.
May those who try to destroy me
  be humiliated and put to shame.
May those who take delight in my trouble
  be turned back in disgrace.
Let them be horrified by their shame,
  for they said "Aha! We've got him now!"

But may all who search for you
  be filled with joy and gladness in you.
May those who love your salvation
  repeatedly shout, "The LORD is great!"
As for me, since I am poor and needy,
  let the Lord keep me in his thoughts.
You are my helper and my savior.
  O my God, do not delay.

Think deeply about what you just read. Use all your senses, emotions, and imagination to interact with this psalm. Feel free to underline words or doodle or write.

Respond to all you've received. Compile your thoughts, and turn them into a prayer to God. Start with this prayer, and add to it to create your own. Pray aloud or silently, alone or with others.

Lord, in such an instant society, it's hard to patiently wait on You. Help me trust Your timing, knowing it is far better than my own. May I not take matters into my own hands, because You're far more capable of holding all things.

I confess that there are people I have a hard time forgiving. Yet You command me to. Help me recall Your forgiveness and extend that same grace to those around me. I want to earnestly live out Your command so that I may walk in freedom.

Bring to my mind now any foothold I have given or false agreements I've made with the Devil. Break those in Your name, Jesus. May I walk in the freedom You have offered me through the cross and Your resurrection. I choose now to serve You as King of Kings and Lord of Lords.

Thank You for offering me freedom and victory in Jesus.

In Jesus' name I pray, amen.

Personal Psalm Writing

Use this space to write your own psalm based on your current situation and prayers. Get creative!

WHO IS GOD?

Our God is the breath of this world. When you follow Him, you follow the Creator of all we are. Men can play with swords and crowns and words like treason. But God brings life to all. And He is the great author of the story. So let Him write it.

HILA, SEASON 1, EPISODE 3, HOUSE OF DAVID

"Don't be afraid!" David said. "I intend to show kindness to you because of my promise to your father, Jonathan. I will give you all the property that once belonged to your grandfather Saul, and you will eat here with me at the king's table!"

2 SAMUEL 9:7

GOD IS TRUE TO HIS WORD

Once upon a time, there was a little girl who grabbed her crayons and a piece of paper. She declared to her mom, "I'm going to draw a picture of God." Mom replied, "Honey, nobody knows what God looks like." The girl was undeterred. "They will when I'm done."

This story makes us wonder, what does God look like? What is God like? Is He smiling or frowning? Is He approachable or not? Does He approve or disapprove of us? Who is God?

Take a moment, like the little girl in the story, to doodle a picture of God, or write down some adjectives you think describe His character. Get creative!

Throughout history, people have been asking the above questions about God. We've tried to define the Almighty. We've even projected images of people or things we're familiar with onto our definition of God. However, we cannot compare anyone or anything we know to God because we are all flawed. There is no one and nothing like the Lord, so it is incredibly important that we know Him personally.

Look at Psalm 86:8–10, and fill in the blanks.

No pagan god is like you, O Lord.
_____ can do what you do!
All the nations you made
will come and _____ before you, Lord;
they will _____ your holy name.

For you are _____ and perform
_____ deeds.
You _____ are God.

To get a really good view of God, we can look at how He is presented in Scripture. Jesus gives us a picture of God in His parable about the prodigal son. Open your Bible to Luke 15:11–24, and answer the following questions:

How many sons did the man have?

What did the younger son ask his father?

What did the father do?

When the younger son came to his senses, what did he decide to do?

DIRECTOR'S CUT: RECAP

We've come so far in our Bible study. Let's pause for a moment and recap how we got to this very moment in the life of David.

Israel wanted a king. Despite the fact that God had led them in the past by means of prophets and judges, the people said, "No, we don't want that anymore. All the other nations have a king. We want one too." So the Lord gave them exactly what they wanted: a king after the people's heart. Saul was tall, good-looking, and charismatic and had all the credentials to be a successful politician. However, he used his throne to glorify himself and as a result became paranoid, jealous, and murderous. So the Lord rejected Saul as king.

Then the Lord told the prophet Samuel to go to the little town of Bethlehem and find a man named Jesse, because out of his household God was going to select the next king of Israel. So Samuel showed up, and the seven sons of Jesse were paraded before the visiting prophet. And the Lord said, "None of them are my choice." Jesse reluctantly acknowledged that he had one more son out in the field watching the sheep.

That shepherd, of course, was David. Young David came in, and

How did the father react when he saw his son returning home?

What did the son say to his father?

What did the father reply?

What did the household do upon the younger son's return?

What do you think this parable reveals about the character of God?

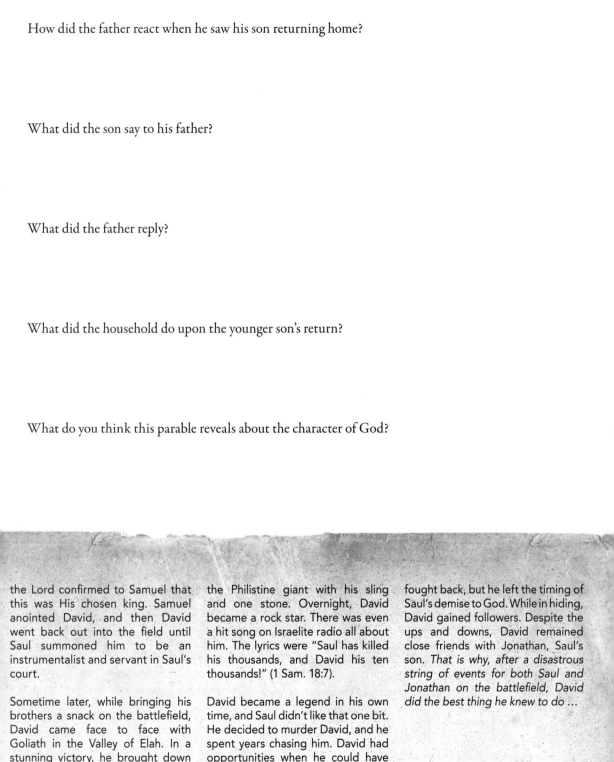

the Lord confirmed to Samuel that this was His chosen king. Samuel anointed David, and then David went back out into the field until Saul summoned him to be an instrumentalist and servant in Saul's court.

Sometime later, while bringing his brothers a snack on the battlefield, David came face to face with Goliath in the Valley of Elah. In a stunning victory, he brought down the Philistine giant with his sling and one stone. Overnight, David became a rock star. There was even a hit song on Israelite radio all about him. The lyrics were "Saul has killed his thousands, and David his ten thousands!" (1 Sam. 18:7).

David became a legend in his own time, and Saul didn't like that one bit. He decided to murder David, and he spent years chasing him. David had opportunities when he could have fought back, but he left the timing of Saul's demise to God. While in hiding, David gained followers. Despite the ups and downs, David remained close friends with Jonathan, Saul's son. *That is why, after a disastrous string of events for both Saul and Jonathan on the battlefield, David did the best thing he knew to do ...*

According to Jesus, God is a father who longs for fellowship with us, misses us when we are gone, and will forgive us of our sin. Let's also take a moment to observe His character in the Old Testament, because He is the same yesterday, today, and forever (see Heb. 13:8). *We have a beautiful picture of God in the Old Testament in the story of David and Mephibosheth.*

If you remember, David had a feeling that something was up with Saul. His friend, Prince Jonathan, helped him by telling him of his father's plan to murder David and by sending him out to find safety. Before the friends parted ways, they made a promise.

Look up 1 Samuel 20:41–42, and write down what Jonathan said to David.

This would be the last time these best friends would see each other. As soon as David departed from this conversation, he went into hiding for years, gained a following, started a small army, defeated the Philistines and Amalekites, married two women, started families, and began his rise to power. Things were looking up for David. Meanwhile, another war against the Philistines delivered the fatal blow to the house of Saul.

Open your Bible to 1 Samuel 31:1–6. What happened to Saul and his sons?

Tragically, in the same battle in which King Saul died, Jonathan's life was taken as well. David learned of the news from a messenger. He and his entire army mourned the loss of his best friend, of the king, and of his family. The Lord then sent David to the town of Hebron, where the Israelites anointed him as the new king.

It wasn't all rainbows and sunshine after Saul died, though. David still had to defeat Saul's remaining sons for the throne. This established the beginning of David's official reign as Israel's leader. Even with all his success, David never forgot that last promise he made to Jonathan. He gave Jonathan his word that he would be loyal to their relationship throughout generations, and he intended to keep it.

Looking at 2 Samuel 9:1–4, fill in the blanks:

David asked, "Is anyone in Saul's family still alive—anyone to whom I can show _____ for Jonathan's sake?" He summoned a man named Ziba, who had been one of Saul's servants. "Are you Ziba?" the king asked.

"Yes sir, I am," Ziba replied.

The king then asked him, "Is anyone still alive from Saul's family? If so, I want to show God's _____ to them."

Ziba replied, "Yes, one of Jonathan's _____ is still alive. He is crippled in both feet."

"Where is he?" the king asked.

Like God, David was a man of his word. After coming to power, David could have just moved on. No one would ever have known that he'd never followed through on his oath to Jonathan. Instead, he made good on his promise by extending lavish kindness to Jonathan's son, Mephibosheth.

What radical grace! It points us toward God's own heart for keeping His word with us. Like Mephibosheth, we, too, have sinned against the King of Kings. We, too, have done things that separate us from God's kingdom. However, through Christ's death and resurrection, God has restored our relationship with Him. As David did for Mephibosheth, so God offers us access to His riches, a seat at His table, and a home with Him. Throughout Scripture, God promises His people many incredible things.

MEPHIBOSHETH
son of Jonathan
disabled in his legs
lost everything
restored by David

Look up the following verses, and identify the promises from God:

Romans 5:8

John 10:28

1 John 1:9

1 Corinthians 2:9

Psalm 18:2

Ephesians 1:3–4

Romans 8:28

Jeremiah 29:11

John 3:16

John 14:2

Which of these promises means the most to you right now? Why?

The relationship between David and Mephibosheth offers us an example of this truth about God: "If we are unfaithful, he remains faithful, for he cannot deny who he is" (2 Tim. 2:13). No matter what, God is seeking us out. He wants to bless us with an incredible inheritance, and He has never broken His word. Just as David's promises were true for Mephibosheth, God's promises will always be true for us.

GOD FORGIVES

After the American Civil War was over, President Abraham Lincoln wanted to reunite America, so he extended mercy to his enemies. Someone asked why he made friends with his adversaries instead of destroying them. Lincoln responded, "Do I not destroy my enemies when I make them my friends?"[1]

David could have sought justice and engaged in payback. He had been hurt by Saul. He'd been terrorized and hunted for years. Driven from his wife and his home. He could have killed any descendants he found who belonged to the house of Saul because they were threats to his throne. David, however, not only forgave, but he also extended kindness. *David seemed to know that we destroy our enemies when we make them our friends.*

Read 2 Samuel 9:8–13, and answer the following questions:

What did Mephibosheth call himself?

BREAKING THE FOURTH WALL

I was overjoyed when I learned about Mephibosheth. Jonathan's legacy lived on! And, though his soul had departed from this earth, it brought me peace to know that Jonathan had a living son. This was my chance to make good on my promise to honor him. I didn't get to say goodbye to my best friend, but I could welcome his family into my kingdom.

When I asked about Saul's family, I used the word *kindness*, a word that often pops up in Scripture. It's not because I wanted to be exceptionally friendly. God's kindness goes beyond just being nice. I wanted to mirror the character of God to Jonathan's son by being radically compassionate in the same way that the Lord had been so generous to me.

As the new king, I could have viewed Jonathan's heir as my enemy. However, I wanted the entire world to know that we were friends.

After reading these stories, what do you think God looks like? How is that different from the way you answered this question at the beginning of the lesson?

What does it mean to you that God is true to His word?

When the king summoned Ziba, what did he tell Ziba he offered to Mephibosheth?

Mephibosheth ate at David's table like a what? How often?

Mephibosheth was only five years old when his father and grandfather were killed on the battlefield. Up until then, he was a prince and probably had a pretty great life. Everything was going his way until the news came that Saul and Jonathan had been killed.

Look up 2 Samuel 4:4. What does this verse reveal happened to Mephibosheth? Who dropped him and why?

All of a sudden, Mephibosheth went from royalty to outcast. He was considered an enemy of King David because he was of Saul's bloodline. Also, in the ancient world, to be both lame and without privilege could have been a death sentence, especially for a young boy. Mephibosheth was dropped, all right—not only physically but also culturally, financially, and personally.

Maybe you can sympathize. Through no fault of your own, bad things happened in your childhood or to your family. Events transpired that didn't seem fair, especially when you compared your life to the lives of others. The rug was pulled out from underneath you, and you aren't sure you'll ever regain right standing with others or with God.

Recall a time when you felt "dropped." What happened? How did you feel as a result? How did you react?

What we need to know is this: God specializes in taking people who have been "dropped" in life and picking them up again. He also specializes in offering forgiveness and lifting up the lowly.

Mephibosheth was probably angry at David. Maybe he even blamed his lameness and grief on the new king. He possibly thought, *This isn't fair. I would be on the throne right now if it weren't for him.* He was probably living in fear that someday there would be a knock at the door and the soldiers of David would drag him out and execute him. Why would he fear that? Because that's how kings did things back then. And because he didn't know David at all. He had no idea the king wanted to offer him forgiveness and grace.

We also often make wrong assumptions about God. We think He's up in Heaven wagging His finger in disapproval of us when we make a mistake. When bad things happen, we presume God is simply giving us what we deserve. But that's just not true.

Open your Bible to Ephesians 1:7 and 2:8–9, and fill in the blanks:

> He is so rich in kindness and _____ that he purchased our _____ with the blood of his Son and _____ our sins.

> God _____ you by his _____ when you believed. And you can't take credit for this; it is a _____ from God. Salvation is not a _____ for the good things we have done, so none of us can boast about it.

In these biblical references, *grace* is synonymous with the kindness David wanted to offer Mephibosheth. It

BREAKING THE FOURTH WALL

I did wonder for a minute what would happen if Mephibosheth rejected my invitation. He could have held me responsible for his father's death. He could have taken after his grandfather and hated my guts. I don't see how anyone would, but he could have preferred Lo Debar or been too fearful to leave.

As I saw him limp into the palace, I felt relieved. He had come home. When I noticed the glint of fear in his eyes, I had to set him at ease and reveal my heart to him. I repeated to him a phrase that I know occurs hundreds of times in the Bible: "Don't be afraid." Once he got to know me, Mephibosheth knew there was nothing to be scared of. I longed to see him restored. When I told him he would always eat at my table, his eyes brightened. He, too, was relieved. Those final words sealed the deal: Mephibosheth was here to stay. Praise God!

What does it mean to you that God has extended an invitation for you to sit at His table?

What have David's actions in this passage and his heart toward Mephibosheth revealed to you about the character of God?

means "unmerited favor."[2] Imagine the shock Mephibosheth experienced when he discovered that David didn't want to kill him but instead wanted to extravagantly bless him. David didn't desire for Mephibosheth to be an outcast but a son sitting at his table. We experience the same wild realization Mephibosheth did when we discover God's forgiveness and grace.

God's kindness is abundant. When Jesus died on the cross for our sins, He offered salvation for all who would believe. As a result, God seeks us out, knocks on the door of our heart, and, in place of His judgment and wrath, surprises us with grace and mercy.

When we look at Colossians 1:21–22, we see that we are no longer enemies of God. According to John 15:15, what does He call us instead?

God longs for us to receive His free gift of forgiveness and salvation through Christ. His heart is set on lifting up all who have been knocked down in life. He's never merely holding back the judgment that we deserve but is instead extending to us His unmerited favor and the opportunity to live as sons and daughters with full access to His heavenly kingdom.

CLOSE-UP

Living in Old Testament times, David didn't get to meet the Messiah. It wasn't until generations later that Joseph would be born into his family line and be chosen to be the earthly father figure to Jesus. David had to make sacrifices to atone for his sin, but we now get to freely accept God's forgiveness. What abounding grace and mercy we all get to receive because of Jesus' sacrifice on the cross! What a miracle!

As we look back at the time David lived in, we may feel that God was more judgmental and full of wrath then. However, David experienced God as a friend. God drew near to him in all his hardship. His presence was ever with David and guided him. Even when David made mistakes, God was gracious to forgive him and help him get his life back on track.

As David got to know Mephibosheth and learned of the way he was dropped as a child, David knew God wanted to pick him back up. So David elevated the young man in his kingdom and gave him a seat at the king's table every day. He received his father's inheritance. Just as God had given so much to David, so it was his turn to give it away.

Do you typically view God as judgmental or full of grace and forgiveness? Why do you think that is?

While David was not perfect in the way that God is perfect, God did inspire his actions. How do you think radical kindness reflects God's character?

Though David hadn't been physically dropped, he could sympathize with Mephibosheth in the way he was sent to the bottom of the ladder in his family and shunned and hunted by Saul. Mephibosheth had physical wounds, and David had internal ones. As they sat together at the table, I imagine there were nights when they discussed the way that God had lifted them both back up. God had brought them so far.

What about you? How has God lifted you back up?

GOD GRANTS US ALL A SEAT AT HIS TABLE

Let's look again at 2 Samuel 9:4–5. Where did Mephibosheth live? Lo Debar was an obscure spot on the east side of the Jordan River. It was known for being a dry, barren field in the middle of nowhere. In fact, the very name Lo Debar means "a place of no pasture."[3]

We've all lived in Lo Debar at one time or another, haven't we? We've lacked direction in life and felt paralyzed as a result. Maybe there's a prayer we've been praying for so long we think God doesn't hear us or has deserted us. Our souls have felt weary and dry after a long and hard season when nothing we tried to plant ever grew. We have felt low, unloved, unwanted, undeserving, or unneeded.

What was it like in your own version of Lo Debar? If it were a real place, how would you describe it? Do you feel like you're living there right now?

Just as David reached out to Mephibosheth, so God reaches out to us.

Look at what David did in verse 5. He sent for Mephibosheth and brought him from Lo Debar into his palace. David was persistent, modeling God's character by being willing to bring his friend-to-be into a place of safety and provision.

Notice Mephibosheth's reaction in verses 6–7. How did he feel when he was brought into David's presence? What did David say to him?

Leaving Lo Debar can seem scary. I'm sure it was terrifying for Mephibosheth because he probably had no idea what he was in for when he showed up on David's doorstep. Was this an ambush? A cruel joke? Also, we can get used to the desert. It takes some courage to pack up the baggage of our lives and approach God. However, moving toward His presence is always the best step we can take.

A. W. Tozer said, "Nothing twists and deforms the soul more than a low or unworthy conception of God."[4]

If he had known David, Mephibosheth would not have been afraid. He would have understood that David was a man after God's own heart. In the same way, we can be afraid of God because we have a warped view of who He is. We can stay stuck in the desert, not knowing that He's offered us a home in a land of abundance, provision, and blessing. Not knowing that we don't have to be afraid of God.

One of the most outstanding spots in 2 Samuel 9 is where it says, "Mephibosheth ate regularly at David's table, like one of the king's own sons" (v. 11). The fact that Mephibosheth ate at David's table is mentioned four times in just thirteen verses in this chapter. The author clearly wanted to drive home this fact. But why?

Because God is offering us the same invitation: a seat at His table.

Read Psalm 23 and fill in the blanks.

> You prepare a _____ for me
>   in the presence of my enemies.
> You honor me by _____ my head with oil;
>   my cup _____ with blessings. (v. 5)

Psalm 23 is a heartfelt poem by King David. He would have known the table as a symbol of family, nourishment, and community. He, too, had been an enemy and an outcast. He understood what it meant to have a seat at God's table even when he was at his lowest points in life. He was blessed even while Saul was cursing him. So he empathized with Mephibosheth and raised him up by giving him a chair at the king's own table.

Mephibosheth could have refused and said, "I'm not going to that palace. I'm not going to sit at his table. I don't want any of it. I want to stay here in Lo Debar and watch the tumbleweeds blow by." Instead, he decided to go—and was delighted when he was invited to sit at that table.

In the same way, we don't have to say yes to Jesus Christ. We can live the way we want and face the consequences of it. Or we can accept God's invitation to "taste and see that the LORD is good" (Ps. 34:8). We can come to His table, be His sons and daughters, and live in the spiritual provision and freedom we've always longed for.

David's Diary

Slowly and reflectively read the following psalm aloud.

Psalm 145

I will exalt you, my God and King,
    and praise your name for ever and ever.
I will praise you every day;
    yes, I will praise you forever.
Great is the LORD! He is most worthy of praise!
    No one can measure his greatness.

Let each generation tell its children of your mighty acts;
    let them proclaim your power.
I will meditate on your majestic, glorious splendor
    and your wonderful miracles.
Your awe-inspiring deeds will be on every tongue;
    I will proclaim your greatness.
Everyone will share the story of your wonderful goodness;
    they will sing with joy about your righteousness.

The LORD is merciful and compassionate,
    slow to get angry and filled with unfailing love.
The LORD is good to everyone.
    He showers compassion on all his creation.
All of your works will thank you, LORD,
    and your faithful followers will praise you.
They will speak of the glory of your kingdom;
    they will give examples of your power.
They will tell about your mighty deeds
    and about the majesty and glory of your reign.
For your kingdom is an everlasting kingdom.
    You rule throughout all generations.

The LORD always keeps his promises;
    he is gracious in all he does.
The LORD helps the fallen
    and lifts those bent beneath their loads.
The eyes of all look to you in hope;
    you give them their food as they need it.
When you open your hand,
    you satisfy the hunger and thirst of every living thing.
The LORD is righteous in everything he does;
    he is filled with kindness.
The LORD is close to all who call on him,
    yes, to all who call on him in truth.
He grants the desires of those who fear him;
    he hears their cries for help and rescues them.
The LORD protects all those who love him,
    but he destroys the wicked.

I will praise the LORD,
    and may everyone on earth bless his holy name
    forever and ever.

Think deeply about what you just read. Use all your senses, emotions, and imagination to interact with this psalm. Feel free to underline words or doodle or write.

Respond to all you've received. Compile your thoughts, and turn them into a prayer. I will start, and then you can use the rest of the space to run with your own. Pray aloud or silently, with others or in your prayer closet.

> *God, we want to know You and not just know about You.*
> *Thank You for using David's relationship with Mephibosheth to*
> *reveal different aspects of Your character. You are always true*
> *to Your word, full of forgiveness, and abounding in grace.*
>
> *Thank You that You have an open-door policy for our rela-*
> *tionship. We can come to You just as we are, whenever and*

wherever. So we take this moment to acknowledge that You have pursued us. You have sought us out and invited us by name into Your presence. You lift us up, even in our lowest points in life. Thank You for never giving up on us.

May we continue to learn more and more about You by spending time in Your Word. Illuminate Your heart for us as we continue in this Bible study. We join You at Your table today to fellowship with You, ask You questions, and enjoy all the provisions of Heaven that we have access to as sons and daughters of the King.

In Jesus' name I pray, amen.

Personal Psalm Writing

Following David's "I'm-struggling-and-yet-I-trust" pattern, use this space to write your own psalm based on your current situation and prayers. Pour your heart out.

THE GOD OF SECOND CHANCES

Secrets are heavy, David. Do you have any?
MYCHAL, SEASON 1, EPISODE 5, HOUSE OF DAVID

Then David confessed to Nathan, "I have sinned against the LORD." Nathan replied, "Yes, but the LORD has forgiven you, and you won't die for this sin. Nevertheless, because you have shown utter contempt for the word of the LORD by doing this, your child will die."... Then David got up from the ground, washed himself, put on lotions, and changed his clothes. He went to the Tabernacle and worshiped the LORD. After that, he returned to the palace and was served food and ate.
2 SAMUEL 12:13–14, 20

WHEN WE NEED RESTORATION AFTER A FALL

Have you ever messed up horribly in life? Of course you have. Me too. We've all made mistakes. We all have sinned. No exceptions. We have sunk so low, we thought we couldn't go any lower. But there's good news! We serve a God who gives second, third, and fourth chances.

Now, that does not mean that we can sin with abandon and not face consequences. Sometimes we think that because God forgives, we can go out and do whatever we want. So long as we say "I'm sorry," everything's cool. If you repent before God and ask for His forgiveness, you are forgiven, of course, but there might be repercussions.

For example, let's say you decide to rob a bank this afternoon. You walk in, hold up the bank, and steal the money. As you're walking out, you're arrested, and you say, "Oh, God, forgive me." You're definitely forgiven, but you're still going to jail.

What does Galatians 6:7–9 say about the consequences of our actions?

Well, here before us now in our Bible study is the story of a king who decided to sow some bad seeds that grew into weeds of sin and regret. And afterward, our main character desperately needed forgiveness.

David was an incredible leader who lived a godly life for the first twenty years of his reign as Israel's king. At age fifty, though, something began to go amiss. It started with a lustful look, and it became a nationwide scandal with repercussions that lasted the rest of his life. Even when you've been walking with the Lord for a long time, you still are vulnerable to falling.

Look up 1 Corinthians 10:12. What does this verse warn us about?

Here's how David's downturn started:

> In the spring of the year, when kings normally go out to war, David sent Joab and the Israelite army to fight the Ammonites. They destroyed the Ammonite army and laid siege to the city of Rabbah. However, David stayed behind in Jerusalem.
>
> Late one afternoon, after his midday rest, David got out of bed and was walking on the roof of the palace. As he looked out over the city, he noticed a woman of unusual beauty taking a bath. He sent someone to find out who she was, and he was told, "She is Bathsheba, the daughter of Eliam and the wife of Uriah the Hittite." Then David sent messengers to get her; and when she came to the palace, he slept

with her. She had just completed the purification rites after having her menstrual period. Then she returned home. Later, when Bathsheba discovered that she was pregnant, she sent David a message, saying, "I'm pregnant." (2 Sam. 11:1–5)

Looking at the highlighted areas, what stands out to you most? Why?

If it was "the time when kings go to war," why wasn't King David out there with the army? In the opening scene, we see David standing in the wrong place at the wrong time. He's not fighting in a war; he's taking a nap and strolling on the rooftop.

Now, David is at the age when people may have a so-called midlife crisis. I don't know how much I really believe in this phenomenon. We don't read that David got a red hot-rod chariot or anything. Personally, I think something like this could happen at any age or stage of life. What we do know is that he's idle when he should have been busy, and this is really where the sin all started.

David had been on a roll up to this point, leading his country to victory in every battle and always giving glory to God. But then, after decades of great success, David became comfortable and caved in when the Devil presented him with temptation.

FORESHADOWING

Centuries later, Jesus was also tempted by the Devil in a moment of weakness. He had been fasting for forty days when Satan started mocking Him by extending an invitation to eat. The offerings only got more enticing from there. However, Jesus reacted differently than David did. Take a moment to examine how this tactic from the Enemy played out even for Jesus, and make notes on how David should have responded to his own temptations.

Matthew 3:16—4:11

Jesus was attacked by Satan right after His baptism. After the dove came the Devil. After the blessing came the attack. The two often go hand in hand. The Devil waits for the moment when he thinks we're the most vulnerable, when we might lower our guard spiritually, and then he moves in.

Where David responded to temptation out of his own wants and desires, Jesus countered temptation with God's Word. He resisted the Devil. He didn't fall for Satan's sneaky ways. As a result, Satan left him, and angels came to attend to Him.

David's comfort led him to compromise. The tale of David and Bathsheba is a warning to us all to stay spiritually alert and to stand firmly on God's Word. When temptations inevitably come, we must seek to avoid them at all costs.

Look at 1 Peter 5:10, and fill in the blanks:

> In his _____
> God called you to share his eternal glory
> by means of Christ Jesus. So after you have
> _____ a little
> while, he will _____,
> _____, and
> _____ you, and he will
> place you on a firm foundation.

While the consequences of our wrongdoing may remain, 1 Peter 5:10 reminds us that suffering is temporary. When we seek Christ and start to walk in His ways again, He begins to rebuild our character and reputation. Where we are weak, He can make us strong. If the foundations of our faith have been shaken, He can make them firm. When we repent, Jesus will forgive us for all the ways we haven't remained loyal to Him, and He will empower us to be steadfast again in our pursuit of what is holy and true. *Restoration can come after any fall ... if we seek God for it and act in accordance with His Word.*

DIRECTOR'S CUT: THE VIEW FROM THE PALACE

David's palace wasn't what we typically think of as a castle with gigantic sloped roofs and tall pointed pillars. Just outside the walls of the city of David, on Mount Zion, would have been an impressive structure with long stone walls, a grand entrance, and guard towers. Aside from a courtyard on the ground level, David's palace would have also had a terrace on a flat roof, kind of like our modern concept of a patio.[1] From there, David could have seen everything going on in his city ... including a woman of unusual beauty taking a bath.

Second Samuel 11 lacks details when it comes to Bathsheba's side of the story. Where was she bathing? Did she want David to see her, or was she an innocent victim who was taken advantage of by the king? We can only speculate. Most likely, Bathsheba was bathing in what she assumed was a private space outside of her home, not thinking the king would be on his roof when he should have been off to war. Many scholars think that when David saw her from his terrace, it was pure chance. However, it quickly became an incident he couldn't forget.[2]

WHEN OUR PAST SINS HAVE PRESENT CONSEQUENCES

David didn't fall suddenly. As with everyone, it was a process. Second Samuel 5:13 tells us, "After moving from Hebron to Jerusalem, David married more concubines and wives, and they had more sons and daughters." David was living in direct disobedience to God because he took concubines. A concubine is basically a mistress. And he had quite a few of them. He was indulging himself and living immorally before God.

Sometimes we think we can make a few compromises here and there and it won't come back to bite us. *But sin always has consequences.*

Have any of your small sins led to big problems? What happened? How did your decisions come back to bite you?

BREAKING THE FOURTH WALL

No, I'm not proud of my actions in this part of my life. Where before I was reflecting the character of God, here I began to indulge the desires of my flesh. I caved into lust when I was presented with temptation. It's hard for me to look back on it all. I'd love your take on these questions:

Why do you think the Devil tries to follow success with temptation?

Comparing my response to Jesus' in Matthew 3:16—4:1–11, what do you think I should have done?

Are there areas of success in your life where you should take extra precautions to ensure that the Devil doesn't tempt you or trip you up?

David slowly turned away from the Lord as he let lust into his heart ... a few small decisions at a time. He probably assumed that the next woman would fulfill his desires. If not her, then the next. However, his sin never satisfied him.

We cannot feed our sin, because that is like going to a Mexican restaurant when we're incredibly hungry, sitting down with chips and queso, and stuffing our faces as the server continually brings out more baskets of chips. Although the chips fill our stomachs, we don't feel satisfied. Gorging ourselves prevents us from enjoying the real reason we came—to savor a flavorful, satisfying meal! In the same way, we can stuff ourselves with everything the world offers but wind up completely discontented. The only thing we'll be full of is regret.

Consider Jesus' words about how He satisfies our souls in John 6:26–40, and answer these questions:

What did Jesus instruct His disciples to work for?

What did they ask in response?

Who did Jesus declare that He was?

What will those who come to Him never experience?

What you feed will grow. When our past sin begins to lead to present problems, we must starve it and allow it to die. David should have stopped adding concubines and wives and instead searched for God to satisfy the longings of his heart. He was looking for an earthly solution for a spiritual problem. We, too, cannot feed our bodies their desires and whims and think they will quench the part of our souls that needs to be filled with the Bread of Life.

Look at 1 John 1:9. If we confess our sins, what will God do?

When we become aware that we've allowed sin to infiltrate our lives, we can begin to remove its foothold by confessing it to Jesus.

Another word we commonly use here is *repentance*, which means "the act of changing one's mind."[3] This isn't a simple, "I'm sorry, Jesus." It's a firm decision to view our sin as actions and thoughts that directly hurt God's heart. To walk in freedom from past sin, we must begin to walk in a brand-new direction. *As we take steps toward Jesus, we will find that our past doesn't dictate our present and that grace and mercy are gifts offered to us if we'll receive them here and now.*

CLOSE-UP

If David could give us any advice right now, I assume it would be, "Don't look for an earthly solution to your spiritual problems." David had a lust issue and kept trying to fill it with more wives and concubines. It was truly a pit that, no matter how much dirt and rocks he poured into it, remained bottomless. I don't think he would recommend his approach.

Based on the Scriptures you've looked up, what advice would you have given David the moment he saw Bathsheba? What do you think he should have done?

David felt empty. That's why it's so important that Jesus would later call Himself the Bread of Life. How wonderful for God's people that we can seek satisfaction in Jesus!

What's your take? Why do you think Jesus called Himself the Bread of Life in John 6? What does that mean to you?

Learn from David's mistakes. Admit what you're struggling with. Catch the sin before it bites you by considering the following question: Do you need to confess and repent of any past sin so that you can walk forward in the freedom Christ offers you?

WHEN YOU NEED TO RETURN AFTER A SPIRITUAL VACATION

David was sleeping when he should have been fighting.

While his men were at war, David was kicking back and taking some time off. Now, there is nothing wrong with this when it comes to work-life rhythms. However, it seems that David was displaying physically what he was secretly doing spiritually. He had become lazy in his relationship with God. He was taking a spiritual vacation.

Spiritual rest is very different from spiritual laziness. Spiritual rest comes while staying in the fight but pausing to take moments like that described in Mark 6:31.

In this verse, what did Jesus say to the apostles? Where did they go in response?

Jesus pulled His disciples away from the crowd to rest but never told them to leave Him. He invited them to rest in Him. God is rest. We don't recharge by leaving Him behind. We rest spiritually by following Him, even into secret places.

In your own words, what would you say is the difference between enjoying spiritual rest and being spiritually lazy?

Phillips Brooks, author and lyricist of the Christmas hymn "O Little Town of Bethlehem," made this statement:

> Sad will be the day for every man when he becomes absolutely contented with the life that he is living, with the thoughts that he is thinking, with the deeds that he is doing, when there is not forever beating at the doors of his soul some great desire to do something larger, which he knows that he was meant and made to do.[4]

This was true for David. He became overly content with his life, and he lowered his guard. Then into his view came a great temptation: an extraordinarily beautiful woman. And he knew he was the king and could have anything he wanted.

Now you have to admire the boldness of the servant who tells the king, "She is Bathsheba, the daughter of Eliam and the wife of Uriah the Hittite" (2 Sam. 11:3). The servant knows what David's thinking, and he tries to be a voice of reason and restraint. He's reminding him, "She's married, dude. Don't even think about it." Instead of living his convictions and behaving in a way he knew was pleasing to the Lord, David took what wasn't his.

When you're deluded by sin, you don't think clearly. Isn't it amazing how, when our judgment has been clouded, we try to rationalize our sin? We say things like,

BATHSHEBA
stunningly beautiful
married to foreign fighter Uriah
taken by & married to David
mother of Solomon

"Well, I'm just not happy in my marriage anymore."
"I work really hard, so I deserve this."
"Hey, everybody else does it, so why shouldn't I?"
"Look, I'm human like everyone else. Besides, we all make mistakes. Don't judge me."

Do you have a go-to excuse to justify your actions when you sin? What is it?

We can come up with any excuse for our actions, can't we? David did the same. He went on a spiritual holiday and thought he should have whatever he wanted. *However, what we want is rarely what God wants for us. So, when we're presented with temptation, God always provides an out for us.*

Record the words of 1 Corinthians 10:13 in the space below:

We have all made sinful choices, and the hard truth we need to hear is that we could have chosen differently. One biblical figure who did the right thing when temptation came along was Joseph. Consider one episode from his story (in Genesis 39:1–12), and answer the following:

Because the Lord was with Joseph, what did He give him?

What did the Lord do for the household of Potiphar because of Joseph?

Everything Potiphar had was under the care of whom?

How is Joseph described?

Who took notice of Joseph? What did she ask him to do?

How did Joseph reply to Potiphar's wife?

When she caught him by his cloak, what did Joseph do?

Mrs. Potiphar kept hitting on Joseph, day in and day out. Each time he was presented with temptation, he refused it and eventually ran from it. When sin grabs at us and tries to steal our attention, we need to act like Joseph (and not like David) and flee in the other direction.

However, not caving in to temptation is hard, isn't it? Even with food! When the "Hot and Ready" sign comes on at Krispy Kreme, it's almost impossible not to pull in. I know this from personal experience. One time, I was riding my motorcycle and approached that bright-red "Hot and Ready" sign, and, like a fly drawn to the light, I parked my bike and made my way into the shop. I then proceeded to eat eight Krispy Kreme doughnuts and chug a glass of cold milk.

In the moment, it was bliss. However, just a few short minutes later, I was miserable, and my body was going into a food coma. I barely had the wherewithal to get back on my bike and ride home.

I tell you that story because sin is often pleasurable. A spiritual vacation feels good in the moment. It's the consequences that hurt. Eating eight doughnuts is awesome, but it's not worth it in the end. Checking out from what we should do and acting on our passion, desire, or interest instead could be fun in the moment. However, the repercussions are usually guilt or shame (for starters). David knew this firsthand. Instead of owning his sin and doing what he needed to do to fix it, he tried to cover it up.

Read 2 Samuel 11:6–27. Summarize what David chose to do.

URIAH
Bathsheba's husband
elite soldier in David's army
foreigner in Israel (Hittite)
loyal, honorable

Instead of repenting of his sin, David came up with a devious plan to try to make it look like the baby belonged to Uriah. But this loyal soldier, this foreigner from the Hittite kingdom, would not fall into David's scheme. Frustrated, David decided just to have Uriah killed by putting him in an impossible situation in battle.

As if he'd swiped a page out of Saul's playbook from when Saul tried to have the Philistines murder him, David saw a threat to what he wanted and took the life of another man so that he could live the way he wanted. However, he didn't bargain on one thing—in his selfishness, he displeased God. He tells us exactly what this felt like in Psalm 32:3–4. Take a look at those verses, and then fill in the following blanks:

When I refused to _____,
   my body wasted away,
   and I groaned all day long.
Day and night your hand of discipline was _____ on me.
   My strength evaporated like _____ in the
     summer heat.

God disciplines those He loves. The weight of conviction that David felt wasn't a punishment but a sign that God was trying to wake David up from his spiritual slumber. It showed that he was a child of God whom the Lord was trying to bring back into right relationship. David knew this because he also wrote Psalm 23:1–3. Note what he said by filling in the blanks:

The LORD is my

   _____,

  I have _____

   _____.

He lets me rest in green meadows;

  he _____ me beside peaceful

   streams.,

  he _____ my

   strength.

He guides me along right paths

  bringing _____ to

   _____.

BREAKING THE FOURTH WALL

Now, I can't be the only one who has ever become spiritually lazy. It happens to the best of us. Asking questions is the best way to get to know someone, and you've answered quite a few by now about my life. So, as a friend who knows me pretty well, give me your take:

Have you ever felt spiritually lazy like I did? What do you think led me to check out from my convictions?

Why do you think Nathan's analogy in 2 Samuel 12 was so effective for helping me realize my mistakes?

A shepherd had two primary instruments in the tending of sheep: a rod and a staff. David knew from firsthand experience that shepherds both protect and discipline their sheep out of deep care for their flock.

What does Hebrews 12:8 say about why we are disciplined?

Props

What does Proverbs 28:13 say we find after we confess our sins?

No discipline is enjoyable while it's happening, but afterward there's a harvest of right living for those who accept correction from God. We see this in our children, right? If you're a parent, you know that you discipline your children out of love. You want what's best for them. And God wants His very best for us.

If confession leads to mercy, then what happened next for David was the best possible thing: he got busted. Read 2 Samuel 12:1–14, and answer the following:

Whom did the Lord send to David?

Tell Nathan's parable in your own words.

NATHAN
brave prophet
adviser to King David
historian & musician

How did David respond?

Whom did Nathan say the man was? What did Nathan state the Lord had said?

What did David finally confess?

How did Nathan reply?

In 2 Samuel 12:13, we finally see David's confession, "I have sinned against the LORD." This confession is what set David apart from Saul. When Saul was confronted with his sin, he dug his heels in to defend his actions even further. David, on the other hand, came clean, admitted his sin, and repented before God. As a result, David was given a second chance in life. As devastating as some of the repercussions of his sins were, he did make a comeback.

FORESHADOWING

There is a tie-in here with the Christmas story. Just as the prophet Samuel came to find young David in Bethlehem, so we find Jesus born in that same tiny town. Jesus was a direct descendant of David—and Bathsheba. God took two broken people who had sinned greatly and used them to bring the Messiah into the world.

Just as God gave David a second chance, so He also offers us the opportunity to begin a new life.

What does Acts 3:19 say happens when we repent and turn to God?

David was a murderer and adulterer. Yet God forgave him when he repented. Clearly, no amount of vacation time away from living God's way can disqualify us from returning to play a part in His great story. When we are confronted with our sin, we must not dig in our heels but be brokenhearted before the Lord and repent. Like David, we, too, can decide to return to God and spiritually reawaken to the good life He offers us.

David's Diary

Slowly and reflectively read the following psalm aloud.

Psalm 51

Have mercy on me, O God,
    because of your unfailing love.
Because of your great compassion,
    blot out the stain of my sins.
Wash me clean from my guilt.
    Purify me from sin.
For I recognize my rebellion;
    it haunts me day and night.
Against you, and you alone, have I sinned;
    I have done what is evil in your sight.
You will be proved right in what you say,
    and your judgment against me is just.
For I was born a sinner—
    yes, from the moment my mother conceived me.
But you desire honesty from the womb,
    teaching me wisdom even there.

Purify me from my sins, and I will be clean;
    wash me, and I will be whiter than snow.
Oh, give me back my joy again;
    you have broken me—
      now let me rejoice.

Don't keep looking at my sins.
  Remove the stain of my guilt.
Create in me a clean heart, O God.
  Renew a loyal spirit within me.
Do not banish me from your presence,
  and don't take your Holy Spirit from me.

Restore to me the joy of your salvation,
  and make me willing to obey you.
Then I will teach your ways to rebels,
  and they will return to you.
Forgive me for shedding blood, O God who saves;
  then I will joyfully sing of your forgiveness.
Unseal my lips, O Lord,
  that my mouth may praise you.

You do not desire a sacrifice, or I would offer one.
  You do want a burnt offering.
The sacrifice you desire is a broken spirit.
  You will not reject a broken and repentant heart, O God.
Look with favor on Zion and help her;
  rebuild the walls of Jerusalem.
Then you will be pleased with sacrifices offered in the right spirit—
  with burnt offerings and whole burnt offerings.
  Then bulls will again be sacrificed on your altar.

Think deeply about what you just read. Use all your senses, emotions, and imagination to interact with this psalm. Feel free to underline words or doodle or write.

Respond to all you've received. Compile your thoughts, and turn them into a prayer. Start with this prayer, and use the rest of the space to write or draw your own. Pray aloud or silently, with others or alone.

Lord, You are the God of second chances. I am so grateful
that when I fail, You don't disqualify me from following You or

playing a part of Your grand story. Instead, You invite me back the moment I decide to return. Where I have fallen, raise me back up. When my sins compound on top of each other and the consequences seem too much to bear, forgive me and restore my reputation. If I have been spiritually on vacation, awaken my soul to get back to doing Your will and walking in Your way.

May Your Holy Spirit convict me of my sin. Help me see that I need You, Jesus. Set me free so that I can find joy and refreshment in You again. Speak to me now and reveal any area of my life where I need to repent right now. I ask for Your forgiveness and receive the second chance You offer me through the death and resurrection of Jesus Christ.

In Jesus' name, amen.

Personal Psalm Writing

Use this space to write your own psalm based on your current situation and prayers. Get creative!

LEGACY

This is what all men forget. They ask, "Is God for us? Is God with us?" when instead they should ask, "Are we with God?"

SAMUEL, SEASON 1, EPISODE 7, HOUSE OF DAVID

The LORD lives! Praise to my Rock! May God, the Rock of my salvation, be exalted! He is the God who pays back those who harm me; he brings down the nations under me and delivers me from my enemies. You hold me safe beyond the reach of my enemies; you save me from violent opponents. For this, O LORD, I will praise you among the nations; I will sing praises to your name. You give great victories to your king; you show unfailing love to your anointed, to David and all his descendants forever.

2 SAMUEL 22:47–51

DAVID'S LIFE WAS NOT MEASURED BY DURATION BUT DONATION

David is a complex character who accomplished much in his seventy years of life. By the end of his forty-year reign, his people had experienced much success:

- The nation of Israel was unified under one flag.
- Israel had established its capital in Jerusalem.
- The Israelite army was powerful, and they had conquered their great adversaries, the Philistines.
- Righteousness and a hunger for God were prevalent.
- The boundaries of Israel had been extended from six thousand to at least twelve thousand square miles.
- Prosperity had been brought in via extensive trade routes.
- The sounds of the songs and psalms of David could be heard throughout the land.

Read Acts 13:36. How does this verse sum up David's life?

Some Bible translations use the phrase "fell asleep" to describe the death of a godly person.[1] It paints a gentle picture of David, having wrung himself out for God, laying down to rest.

Life is not measured by duration but by donation. David's life and legacy make us ask how our own years will be summarized. What have we given to God? Will it be said of us that we did His will in our generation?

David had a big dream of building a house for the Lord. Up to this point, the Israelites worshipped God in the tabernacle, a portable sanctuary tent. David wanted to give God something permanent and beautiful. So he spent the end of his life saving up all his money and getting the building supplies ready, but the Lord halted his plans. Read 1 Chronicles 28:2–4, and answer these questions:

What did David have it in his heart to build?

BREAKING THE FOURTH WALL

We've made it to the final moments of my life, and, as you can see, I was trying to build God's kingdom until the very end. I didn't always do things right, but I never gave up. So here is my final advice to you: Give all you've got to God, and He will offer you the most blessed and full life. You, too, will reach the end knowing you left it all out on the field. Give the grave nothing.

If you could summarize your thoughts so far, how has my legacy inspired you to serve God?

Take a moment to reflect on your own life. What has the donation of your life been so far? Would you change it? If so, what do you want to be giving back to God and others?

Why did God say he couldn't do it?

From the tribe of Judah, whom did God choose?

We don't usually like it when God says no, do we? Maybe we wanted a certain dream to come true, but it never did. We desired more success, but it never came. We prayed and prayed for something, and it wasn't granted. Sometimes things just don't happen for us. We can never know why God says no.

However, David shows us in this statement to not spend our time focusing on what God didn't do but on all He *has* done throughout our lives. Instead of crying over what didn't happen in his life, David states, "Yet the LORD, the God of Israel, has chosen me" (1 Chron. 28:2–4).

Yet contrasts what comes before it to what comes after it. In our context, this means we carry some burdens, *yet* we've received so many blessings. Take a moment to reflect on the donation of your life. What has God given you? How have you given your life away to others?

Here's my own "Yet Statement":

I am flawed and have experienced great loss and brokenness, yet God has chosen to use me, and I am blessed beyond anything I could ever ask or imagine.

Form your own "Yet Statement" by writing out the following verses to use as examples. Underline the word *yet* or its synonyms when you see them.

Reference	"Yet" Verse
Habakkuk 3:17–18	
Lamentations 3:20–22	
Matthew 6:26	
2 Corinthians 4:16	

In a sense, you've been getting ready for this moment throughout the book as you've written your own personal psalms. Now bring that practice to mind, and use the space below to write your own "Yet Statement":

I love the song "My Testimony" by Elevation Worship. The song says that so long as we're not dead, God's not done with us yet. While we're all still here, on the "earth side" of our heavenly home, we get to choose which side of our "Yet Statement" we will live on. David's legacy challenges us to praise God for the back half. We may not ever gain the world, and things may not go exactly how we want, *yet* we will praise Him. What God has given us and how we gave our blessings away are the best gifts of all.

David Walked Closely with God

After recounting what God had done, David offered his final words of advice to his son and successor, Solomon. Record his statement from 1 Chronicles 28:9–10:

SOLOMON
wisest man ever
son of David & Bathsheba
wrote 3 Bible books
third king of Israel

David used his last speech to urge his son to have an intimate relationship with God. Think about the fact that David, a king who had killed a giant and conquered armies and was one of the most powerful rulers Israel would ever see, a man who had the world at his fingertips, wanted his son to know just how important it is to serve God "with your whole heart."

There are people who know God in the same way they "know" people on social media. They've read about Him and seen some pictures of Him in the way that Christians live or model His love. However, they don't know Him for themselves. This was David's fear for his son. David had made some huge mistakes when he chose his own way over God's, and he didn't want to see Solomon repeat them.

Read David's words in Psalm 27:4, and fill in the blanks:

> The one thing I _____ of the LORD—
>   the thing I _____—
> is to _____ in the house of the LORD
>   all the days of my life,
> _____ in the LORD's perfections
>   and _____ in his Temple.

David desired daily fellowship, intimacy, and closeness with God. This is what sustained him through the most difficult times. In contrast, it was a lack of seeking God and connecting with Him that caused Saul to turn to idolatry, immorality, selfishness, and power. The house of Saul fell because he didn't walk with God. David's willingness to allow God to guide his life made all the difference, sustained his kingdom, and blessed all the people of Israel.

When you are in love with Jesus, you don't want to take a step without Him.

What does 2 Corinthians 5:7 say that Christ followers live by?

This doesn't mean we're blind. This verse describes the unique view we have on life when we allow the Holy Spirit to lead us. As if we've put on a special pair of glasses, we can see the world through God's lens.

I believe David had this unique spiritual outlook because when he messed up, he allowed God to put him back on track. He led Israel with God's own heart. David's life is evidence that the way of freedom becomes plain as we walk with the Lord.

What does Proverbs 3:6 say happens when we acknowledge God?

We find the key to finishing well in Hebrews 12:1–2. What does this verse tell us to strip off? What do we run with? Who should we keep our eyes on?

When we're tempted to think that God's best is less than we hope for, we need to look at God through the lens of David. He avoided becoming a casualty in the spiritual race by running it one mile at a time with God. Yes, he messed up. We will too. However, if we keep our eyes on Jesus, we will finish strong. Run the race with Him.

CLOSE-UP

David knew what finishing strong looked like for him. He wanted to walk closely with God and do all that he could for God with whatever time he had left. Let's make sure our lives are also headed in the right direction by thinking through these questions:

Would you say you walk closely with God and allow Him to guide your life? Or do you more often try to navigate life your own way?

What does it look like for you right now to live by faith and not sight?

How do David's final words to Solomon inspire you to run the race of your life with God? What does finishing strong look like to you?

DAVID WANTED HIS FAMILY TO SERVE GOD FOR GENERATIONS

Let me ask you this hard question: Can your life of following Jesus be held up as a model for the next generation? Can you, like the apostle Paul, say to those coming behind you, "And you should imitate me, just as I imitate Christ" (1 Cor. 11:1)?

David wanted his service to God to be an example that his descendants could follow, and we should want our legacy to be the same. Whether we have biological children or not, we are all setting up how the next generation will view God and impact the world with the love of Jesus.

David's legacy of pursuing God and receiving blessing as a result must have inspired his son, Solomon, because in 1 Kings 3, Solomon receives a dream in which he meets God.

Read 1 Kings 3:1–15, and answer the following:

What did God say to Solomon in the dream?

Whom did Solomon say the Lord had shown great kindness to?

What did Solomon ask God for?

How did God reply? What did He offer Solomon?

If you were Solomon, what would you have asked God for?

Solomon could have asked for the world, but instead he asked for wisdom. Who do you think he learned that from? His dad! He certainly watched his father make decisions for Israel and realized that he would also need knowledge and discernment to lead God's people well. He possibly witnessed his dad writing poetry and heard him humming worship songs as he went about his day. Solomon might have listened to David speak aloud the prayers that realigned his priorities. As the next king of Israel, Solomon would have been taking notes when he heard his dad say things like what he wrote in Psalm 25:1–5.

Read it, and fill in the blanks:

> O LORD, I give my life to you.
>   I _____ in you, my
>   God!
> Do not let me be disgraced,
>   or let my enemies rejoice in my defeat.

BREAKING THE FOURTH WALL

I know this is all a lot to think about. But often, we don't really get the space to plan out how we want our lives to impact others. Take it from me, life is short. You'll blink and be an old man like I was, wanting to go back and pay more attention to your moments and choices. Take this opportunity to get intentional so that you live the full life God desires for you and you're able to leave a legacy that those who come behind you will be proud to inherit. As I leave you on the last pages of this Bible study, I encourage you to reflect on these questions:

What kind of legacy do you want to leave for the rising generations of Christ followers?

What do you think should be different about followers of God? Use Psalm 25:1–5 to help guide your response.

What was your main takeaway from this Bible study? What did God teach you? How will you apply lessons from my life to your own?

No one who _____ in you will ever be

_____,

but disgrace comes to those who try to deceive others.

_____ me the right path, O LORD;

_____ the road for me to follow.

_____ me by your truth and _____ me,

for you are the God who saves me.

All day long I put my _____ in you.

When people observe us, what do you think they see? Are our actions and words inspiring others to seek godly wisdom and insight? Are we mindful of the fact that we are paving the way for the rising generations of followers of Jesus?

While we might not sit on the throne as a king or a queen with an entire nation observing us, we are painting a picture of Christ for the communities around us. Our kids are watching as we open our Bibles, noting that we pray over family decisions, and listening as we turn on worship music in the car. Coworkers are noticing our joy, hard work, and kindness. Friends enter our home and can't quite put their finger on why they love it there or why it feels so safe and inviting. Our cities are blessed by the way the church is coming together to serve those in need.

Props

©imageBROKER/Marén Wischnewski/Getty Images Plus

FORESHADOWING

After Jesus was crucified and resurrected, He made several appearances to His disciples and followers over the course of forty days. He, too, had parting words for His people that still apply to us today. Read His "Great Commission," and note how you think David would have reacted if he'd heard these words from Jesus.

Mark 16:15–19

I imagine that throughout David's life people frequently said, "There's just something different about him." David was born around 1040 BC, began to reign over Israel around 1010 BC, and died in 970 BC.[2] David's life was so set apart that three thousand years later, we're still writing Bible studies about him and learning from his legacy.

What was different about David was that he was a man after God's heart, a king who didn't seek his own glory, and a warrior-poet who was bold enough to stand on Scripture. May we dare, like David, to be different. May we be set apart in our generation so that, from now until eternity, people will still seek and declare the goodness of God.

David's Diary

Slowly and reflectively read the following psalm aloud.

Psalm 72

Give your love of justice to the king, O God,
and righteousness to the king's son.
Help him judge your people in the right way;
let the poor always be treated fairly.
May the mountains yield prosperity for all,
and may the hills be fruitful.
Help him to defend the poor,
to rescue the children of the needy,
and to crush their oppressors.
May they fear you as long as the sun shines,
as long as the moon remains in the sky.
Yes, forever!

May the king's rule be refreshing like spring rain on freshly cut grass,
like the showers that water the earth.
May all the godly flourish during his reign.
May there be abundant prosperity until the moon is no more.
May he reign from sea to sea,
and from the Euphrates River to the ends of the earth.

Desert nomads will bow before him;
    his enemies will fall before him in the dust.
The western kings of Tarshish and other distant lands
    will bring him tribute.
The eastern kings of Sheba and Seba
    will bring him gifts.
All kings will bow before him,
    and all nations will serve him.

He will rescue the poor when they cry to him;
    he will help the oppressed, who have no one to defend them.
He feels pity for the weak and the needy,
    and he will rescue them.
He will redeem them from oppression and violence,
    for their lives are precious to him.

Long live the king!
    May the gold of Sheba be given to him.
May the people always pray for him
    and bless him all day long.
May there be abundant grain throughout the land,
    flourishing even on the hilltops.
May the fruit trees flourish like the trees of Lebanon,
    and may the people thrive like grass in a field.
May the king's name endure forever;
    may it continue as long as the sun shines.
May all nations be blessed through him
    and bring him praise.

Praise the LORD God, the God of Israel,
    who alone does such wonderful things.
Praise his glorious name forever!
    Let the whole earth be filled with his glory.
Amen and amen!

(This ends the prayers of David son of Jesse.)

Think deeply about what you just read. Use all your senses, emotions, and imagination to interact with this psalm. Feel free to underline words or doodle or write.

Respond to all you've received. Take a moment to compile your thoughts and turn them into a prayer to the Lord. Use the space after the prayer to continue writing. You can pray out loud, with others, or silently in your heart.

God, as we recap David's life, it makes us contem-
plate our own legacies. We want to live lives that are
pleasing to You, that are a blessing to others, and that
make a generational impact. We want to make Your name
known above our own accolades or accomplishments.

Show us how we can donate our time and energy to helping
our communities. Open up doors for us to share our faith with
those who don't know you yet. May we draw near to You and
abide in Your presence so that You can guide us down the right
path in life. Help us set up the rising generations for success
when it comes to learning about Your Word, will, and way.

Thank You for this Bible study and all we've learned from
the life of David. Continually bring these lessons to our
minds as we go throughout our days so that we, too, can
leave a legacy as a man or woman after Your heart.

In Jesus' name, amen.

Personal Psalm Writing

Use this space to write your own personal psalm to reflect your current conversations with God.

What Does It Mean to Be a Man or Woman after God's Own Heart?

We Are the House of God

The house of David isn't so unlike our own. Within David's home and family there were ups and downs, joys and sorrows, victories and defeats. One day we're all going to wake up like David did and have more years behind us than ahead of us. His legacy challenges us to live in such a way that we won't say, "Wow, I wasted my life." Rather, may we proclaim, "Serve the Lord!" May we declare to the next generation, "My ceiling is your floor. Take what God gave me, and run with it into the future."

We have two major dates in life: the date of our birth and the date of our death. We don't decide either, but we are radically responsible for what we do with the "dash" in the middle. As we look at the psalms that David penned, knowing his advice would outlive him, we can see that this is what he wanted us all to know how to do: live our dash well. To know God intimately and walk with Him closely as a man or woman chasing after His heart.

> Yet I still belong to you;
> you hold my right hand.
> You guide me with your counsel,
> leading me to a glorious destiny.

Whom have I in heaven but you?
 I desire you more than anything on earth.
My health may fail, and my spirit may grow weak,
 but God remains the strength of my heart;
 he is mine forever. (Ps. 73:23–26)

Christians pray to ask Jesus into their heart. It's wild to think about, but David knew what it was like to have God in his heart long before Jesus ever walked the earth. He knew God as Savior before God sent His Son to die on the cross for our sin. David walked in forgiveness and favor before Jesus rose from the grave to offer new life for all who would believe. David made animal sacrifices at the altar to atone for his sins, but we are the temple of the Holy Spirit, and we have open access to the presence of God. We get to abide with Him in our everyday lives. We all now have the opportunity to have Jesus in our hearts.

We know how dearly God loves us, because he has given us the Holy Spirit to fill
 our hearts with his love. (Rom. 5:5)

We have talked about the house of David, but it's important for us to understand that Christians are the house of God. Our hearts are a home for His love and Spirit.

When we hug a friend, we are inviting them into the house of God.

When we love our families, we are inviting them into the house of God.

When we are talking to our coworkers, we are inviting them into the house of God.

When we are serving members of our community or church, we are inviting them into the house of God.

Wherever we go, God goes with us. The house of God has no walls or boundaries. His doors are wide open for anyone and everyone who will believe. And we, as followers of Christ who are full of His Spirit, are inviting people into the community they long for, the hope they so desperately need, and the life that is everlasting ... simply by showing up and being present.

David's life challenges us to allow God to lead our lives. We can make Him our guide through life's ups and downs by continuing to use the tools we've gained through this study. Keep researching the Scriptures, practicing deep reflection, writing personal psalms, and allowing the characters of the Bible to come to life by using your imagination to put yourself in their shoes. David was a great king, and Jesus is greatest one of all. Let Him rule and reign in your priorities. Invite others to join you as a resident in His kingdom where they can find safety and fulfillment.

We are the house of God because we are men and women after His own heart.

NOTES

LESSON 1: A MAN AFTER GOD'S OWN HEART

1. "David Melech Yisrael," HebrewSongs.com, accessed January 14, 2025, www.hebrewsongs .com/?song=davidmelechyisrael.

2. Allyson Holland, "King David in the Bible—Who Was He? Why Is He Important?," Crosswalk, May 10, 2024, www.crosswalk.com/faith/bible-study/david-in-the-bible-who-was -he-why-is-he-important.html.

3. "1 Samuel 16:6–13 Meaning," The Bible Says, accessed January 9, 2025, https://thebiblesays.com/en/commentary/1sa+16:6.

4. "D. L. Moody," Moody Bible Institute, accessed January 9, 2025, www.moody.edu/about /our-bold-legacy/d-l-moody.

5. Chuck Swindoll, "Humble Appointment," Insight for Living, September 15, 2023, https://insight.org/resources/daily-devotional/individual/humble-appointment2.

6. Mike Reuter, "If Serving Is below You, Leadership Is beyond You," *Three Minute Leadership* (blog), May 17, 2020, https://threeminuteleadership.com/2020/05/17/if-serving-is-below -you-leadership-is-beyond-you.

LESSON 2: HOW TO OVERCOME YOUR GIANTS

1. Tim Chaffey, "Giants in the Bible," Answers in Genesis, February 22, 2012, https://answersingenesis.org/bible-characters/giants-in-the-bible.

2. Alia Hoyt, "At 8 Feet 11 Inches, Robert Wadlow Was the World's Tallest Man," HowStuffWorks, July 22, 2024, https://history.howstuffworks.com/historical-figures/robert -wadlow.htm.

3. Chaffey, "Giants in the Bible."

4. Erich B. Anderson, "Learning from David and Goliath: The True Origin of the Sling Weapon," Warfare History Network, May 2015, https://warfarehistorynetwork.com/article /learning-from-david-gloiath-true-origin-sling-weapon.

5. Lynne Fox, "The Biblical Meaning of Confession," BibleGrapes, 2019, https://biblegrapes.com/the-biblical-meaning-of-confession.

Lesson 3: What to Do When Things Fall Apart

1. Tim Mackie, "David: What's the Big Deal? From No-Name Runt to Celebrated King," BibleProject, May 26, 2017, https://bibleproject.com/articles/david-whats-big-deal.

2. As related in Greg Laurie, *Johnny Cash: The Redemption of an American Icon* (Washington DC: Salem Books, 2022).

3. As related in Laurie, *Johnny Cash.*

4. *Johnny Cash: The Redemption of an American Icon*, directed by Ben Smallbone (Nashville: Kingdom Story Company, 2022).

Lesson 4: What King Will You Follow?

1. C. S. Lewis, *Mere Christianity*, in *The Complete C. S. Lewis Signature Classics* (New York: HarperOne, 2002), 98.

2. David Van Biema, "Should All Be Forgiven?," *Time*, April 5, 1999, https://time.com/archive /6735044/should-all-be-forgiven.

Lesson 5: Who Is God?

1. F. Kathleen Foley, "'Lincoln' Seeks to Set the Facts Straight," *Los Angeles Times*, April 3, 1996, www.latimes.com/archives/la-xpm-1996-04-03-ca-54372-story.html.

2. Billy Graham, "The Unmerited Favor of God," Billy Graham Evangelistic Association, accessed January 14, 2025, https://billygraham.org/devotion/gods-unmerited-favor.

3. Greg Laurie, "Living in Lo-debar," Harvest, July 15, 2014, https://harvest.org/resources /devotion/living-in-lo-debar.

4. A. W. Tozer, *The Root of the Righteous* (Shippensburg, PA: Sea Harp, 2022), chap. 3, www.google.com/books/edition/The_Root_of_the_Righteous_Sea_Harp_Timel /qZSSEAAAQBAJ?hl=en&gbpv=0.

LESSON 6: THE GOD OF SECOND CHANGES

1. Eilat Mazar, "What Did King David's Palace Look Like?," Biblical Archaeology Society, accessed January 10, 2025, https://library.biblicalarchaeology.org/sidebar/what-did-king-davids-palace-look-like.

2. Hilary Lipka, "Was David's Encounter with Bathsheba an Affair or Rape?," Bible Odyssey, accessed January 10, 2025, https://hermeneutics.bibleodyssey.com/articles/was-davids-encounter-with-bathsheba-an-affair-or-rape.

3. "What Does the Bible Say about Repentance?," Got Questions, accessed January 10, 2025, www.gotquestions.org/Bible-repentance.html.

4. *Addresses by the Right Reverend Phillips Brooks* (Boston: Samuel E. Cassino, 1893), 63, www.google.com/books/edition/Addresses_by_the_Right_Reverend_Phillips/yGsNAAAAYAAJ?hl=en&gbpv=0.

LESSON 7: LEGACY

1. Henry M. Morris, "Asleep in Jesus," *Days of Praise*, Institute for Creation Research, March 25, 2024, www.icr.org/article/asleep-jesus.

2. Crystal Hall, "King David of Israel: Overview, Story, and Facts," Study.com, updated November 21, 2023, https://study.com/academy/lesson/king-david-of-israel-history-lesson-quiz.html.

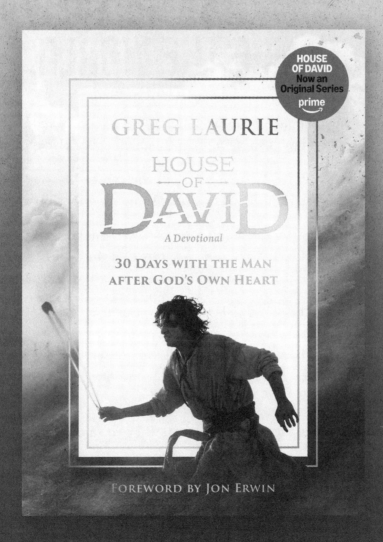

YEARS STRONG

DAVID **C** COOK

JOIN US.
SPREAD THE GOSPEL.
CHANGE THE WORLD.

We believe in equipping the local church with Christ-centered resources that empower believers, even in the most challenging places on earth.

We trust that God is *always* at work, in the power of Jesus and the presence of the Holy Spirit, inviting people into relationship with Him.

We are committed to spreading the gospel throughout the world—across villages, cities, and nations. We trust that the Word of God will transform lives and communities by bringing light to the darkness.

As a global ministry with a 150-year legacy, David C Cook is dedicated to this mission. Each time you purchase a resource or donate, you're supporting a ministry—helping spread the gospel, disciple believers, and raise up leaders in some of the world's most underserved regions.

Your support fuels this mission.
Your partnership sends the gospel where it's needed most.

Discover more. Be the difference.
Visit DavidCCook.org/Donate